THE PROXY CONDITION

How Systems Reshaped Attention, Identity, and What It Means to Be Present

By Harrison Rose Tate

THE PROXY CONDITION

© 2025 Harrison Rose Tate

All rights reserved. No part of this book may be reproduced, stored in a retrieval system, or transmitted by any form or by any means — electronic, mechanical, photocopying, recording, or otherwise — without the prior written permission of the author, except in the case of brief quotations used for review purposes.

Names, identifying details, and select events have been changed for privacy and narrative cohesion.

Published by ECS

Cover design and interior layout by

Harrison Rose Tate

ISBN: 979-8-9987737-4-7
Library of Congress Control Number (LCCN): 2025917730

First Edition

For permissions or inquiries, please contact:

www.harrisonrosetate.com

CONTENTS

PART I: *WHAT HAPPENS WHEN WE OUTSOURCE BEING*

CHAPTER ONE
Your Voice Has Always Been Your Password 1

CHAPTER TWO
My Social Amygdala 13

CHAPTER THREE
Ontological Presence 20

CHAPTER FOUR
A New Taxonomy of Fidelity 29

CHAPTER FIVE
Epistemology 40

CHAPTER SIX
Phenomenology 45

CHAPTER SEVEN
Pragmatism 49

CHAPTER EIGHT
Foundational Traits 51

CHAPTER NINE
Your Brain Has Entered the Chat 59

PART II: *WHERE THE SELVES MET*

CHAPTER TEN
Novelty to Norm 66

CHAPTER ELEVEN
Search Results 72

CHAPTER TWELVE
The Progression 95

CHAPTER THIRTEEN
Selves Gone Rogue 134

PART III: *PROXY MANAGEMENT*

CHAPTER FOURTEEN
Seeing the Cost in Free 145

CHAPTER FIFTEEN
You Are Here, But Also There 161

CHAPTER SIXTEEN
Interior Integration 166

CHAPTER SEVENTEEN
An Infusus Framework 178

CHAPTER EIGHTEEN
The Ethics of Attention 188

CHAPTER NINETEEN
Temporal Jet Lag 201

CHAPTER TWENTY
An Asynchronous Clock 207

CHAPTER TWENTY-ONE
Infusus 214

PART III: *BOTH OF ME*

CHAPTER TWENTY-TWO
The New Authority 222

CHAPTER TWENTY-THREE
The Independent Thinkers in the Room 229

AUTHOR, ACKNOWLEDGEMENTS, INDEXES AND REFERENCES

I Owe You a Beer 245

About the Author's Proxy Self 246

Source Code 247

Index 264

FIGURES

3:1 ORIGINAL REALMS OF ONTOLOGY
Table.. 20

3:2 ONTOLOGICAL PRESENCE
Hierarchical flowchart. 21

3:3 ONTOLOGICAL TEST OF PRESENCE IN THE PROXY CONDITION
Infographic..27

4:1 PRE-PROXY/LEGACY PRESENCE VS. PROXY PRESENCE ACHIEVED
Table.. 33

4:1 PRE-PROXY/LEGACY PRESENCE VS. PROXY PRESENCE ACHIEVED
Table.. 33

4:2 SQL QUERIES ILLUSTRATING BANK EXAMPLE
Code Snippets.. 34

4:3 LAYERS OF PRESENCE IN THE PROXY CONDITION
Infographic 38

6:1 LAYERS OF PHENOMENOLOGY IN THE PROXY CONDITION
Infographic 47

9:1 THE PROXY LINE
Table.. 63

11:1 LEGACY DISTRACTIONS VS. DIGITAL DUALITY
Table.. 86

**12:1 THE ARCHITECTURE OF DIGITAL TRANSFORMATION
1987 TO 1995: INCEPTION**
Table.. 102

**12:2 THE ARCHITECTURE OF DIGITAL TRANSFORMATION
1995 TO 2006: EMERGENCE**
Table.. 105

**12:3 THE ARCHITECTURE OF DIGITAL TRANSFORMATION
2007 TO 2015: EMERGENCE**
Table.. 113

**12:4 THE ARCHITECTURE OF DIGITAL TRANSFORMATION
2016 TO 2020: CONSCIOUSNESS**
Table.. 121

**12:5 THE ARCHITECTURE OF DIGITAL TRANSFORMATION
2021 TO PRESENT: AUTOMATION**
Table.. 126

14:1 HIDDEN COSTS
Table *156*

15:1 PARALLEL PRESENCE: AN EVERYDAY COMPARISON
Graph *163*

16:1 THE FIVE DOMAINS OF TODAY'S COGNITIVE COHERENCE
Venn Diagram *172*

16:2 MODES OF PRESENCE AND PERCEPTION
Infographic *177*

17:1 UNEVOLVED IDENTITY STRUCTURES
Conceptual diagram *180*

17:2 EVOLVING IDENTITY STRUCTURES
Conceptual diagram *181*

17:3 INFUSUS
Conceptual diagram *182*

17:4 STRATIFIED MORALITY
Conceptual diagram *185*

19:1 ESTIMATED IMPACT FELT BY DIGITAL BURNOUT
Table *205*

20:1 MEASURING TIME IN TWO DIMENSIONS
Table *212*

21:1 INFUSUS VS. EXTERIOR CREDIBILITY
Table *216*

21:2 NAVIGATING DIGITAL LIFE
Schematic diagram *218*

21:2 NAVIGATING DIGITAL LIFE WITH INFUSUS
Schematic diagram *220*

23:1 A MUSICAL TUNING FORK
Illustration *230*

23:2 THE NEW COGNITIVE CASTE SYSTEM
Table *228*

23:3 BEHAVIORAL AXIS I: THOUGHT-ORIENTED
Table *237*

23:4 BEHAVIORAL AXIS II: IDENTITY-ORIENTED
Table *238*

23:5 A TYPICAL 1940s SECRETARIAL POOL
Illustration *241*

*If the AI era makes us all-knowing-adjacent,
our new reality is that the general public are now architects,
and the only next-level thinkers will be paradigm framers.*

THE PROXY CONDITION

PART I

*WHAT HAPPENS WHEN
WE OUTSOURCE BEING*

CHAPTER ONE

Your Voice Has Always Been Your Password

**WHEN PRESENCE BECAME DATA,
AND DATA BEGAN TO ACT**

There was always facial recognition. And before artificial intelligence existed, there was, well, *intelligence*. Long before machines could recognize our faces, we built intelligence into every tool we touched.

In many ways, "smart" technology is still dumb. Yes, tech can solve problems we can't, like certain advanced mathematics. But it will be a long time before it catches up to the full range of human capability. As impressive as your phone or your car might be, they are still far from having the level of basic common sense that you do today.

This creates a dichotomy. We adapted years ago to living with technology around us. ChatGPT, maps, calendars and reminders, smart assistants like Alexa or Google Home. Without them, life would seem like the dark ages. We have become reliant on these tools, even when they are invisible. Employers and schools spend millions on systems that allow us to work for *them*. The internet of things (IOT) is taking shape around us. Devices and automation now handle tasks we once did manually, from climate control to robotic vacuuming. They make decisions for us, anticipate our next steps, and adjust options based on our location, memberships, or other inputs.

Voice recognition technologies and biometrics have taken it a step further, integrating tech into the natural flow of our lives.

It has also become our hobby, in the form of social media, gaming, and streaming services. In fact, tech-based hobbies have surpassed all others.

In 2023, Pew Research Center showed that among teens and young adults, playing video games, browsing social media, and watching videos are their top three reported pastimes, exceeding traditional hobbies like sports, reading, or outdoor activities.

In 2024, Statista reported that the top global leisure activities now include streaming video (Netflix, YouTube, TikTok), gaming, browsing social media, and messaging.

In 2024, DataReportal found that the average global internet user spends 6 hours and 40 minutes online daily, with about 2.5 hours of that purely on social media.

In 2023, World Economic Forum noted that digital consumption is now the primary way humans relax, surpassing analog activities for the first time around 2017-2018, but becoming even more dominant post-COVID.

All of this is evidence of an entirely new layer to our existence. We spend our time in a rich, complex, vast environment that **didn't previously exist.**

It's an environment built for convenience, learning, work, laughter and fun. An environment that has made life easier, and better, in many ways. One that exists in every aspect of our life. Many of the results are positive.

But there are drawbacks too. Somehow, this shift has left us restless and unable to feel fully present. Our attention feels divided. To many, the initial sensation presents itself as distraction or fatigue.

That helps explain why some people hate technology.

I'm not one of them. I'm what some would call an early adopter. I've welcomed new tech. I understand its appeal, its power, and its cost. Whether you hate it, love it, or fall somewhere in between, you've probably noticed the feeling. It's difficult to describe. It's all around us.

That may be because we didn't opt into this duality. We were enveloped by it. And our newly-dual selves aren't synchronized. The physical and digital selves will not always align, by design. This mismatch creates a low-grade cognitive dissonance. So we guess:

"Maybe I have ADHD."

"Maybe I'm burnt out."

"Maybe I just can't keep up."

The assumption is that the dissonance came from inside you, but the stimuli that put it there actually originate from something ambient, around you. You're living once, but existing twice.

LIVING TWICE AT ONCE

For the first time in human history, we have two presences. One is the physical body we occupy. The other is digital. Because the digital realm is so vast, the meaning we gather from all of our experiences in it becomes part of our identity.

In her work on *"Triangulating the Self,"* Jenny L. Davis describes how identity is now co-constructed across digital spaces, suggesting coherence emerges as individuals connect disparate experiences into a meaningful whole.

There have always been hints of alternate or virtual presence. The Victorians had calling cards. Renaissance elites had portraits that exaggerated their jawlines. In Medieval times, family crests carried status. Every generation has had versions of a public self, from job interviews to the carefully timed entrance at a dinner party. A photo. A bio.

But those were staged moments, temporary avatars. They didn't interact *back* with us. You put the calling card in a drawer, and you were done. Today, our second presence is persistent. It does not switch off. It is a proxy of us, walking around in a virtual world. It makes friends, gets judged, buys furniture, and misquotes itself in comment sections.

Your physical self sleeps. Your online self does not. It speaks while you dream. It gets tagged in photos you never posed for. It collects data about your behavior and preferences that you didn't know was available.

In the 1960s, Marshall McLuhan wrote that media renders us "essentially discarnate," describing a **self** that exists without a body, stretched across the communications network. His vision was darker than today's reality, but he was definitely on to something.

"Off the grid" used to mean primitive or disconnected. Now it implies peace. Wholeness.

Yet we reach for our phones while lying on the beach in Waikiki. We *choose* the duality.

McLuhan predicted that the medium by which information is delivered would ultimately shape not just how we think, but what we are capable of thinking. He understood that the *form* of communication alters perception more radically than the content ever could.

Dual Self
noun
/ˈd(y)o͞o-əl self/

The co-existence of a physical, embodied identity and a digital, system-recognized proxy. Each will behave differently by design, but both stem from the same core.

A couple of years later, in 1964, when Neil Postman wrote that television had turned everything (including news, politics, and education) into entertainment, he used the only technology available at that time to build upon McLuhan's idea. His main intent was to show how form determines credibility.

HISTORICAL INTERACTIVITY

Among all major social constructs in history, the digital age stands distinctly alone. We are born into race, gender, time, and nationality. Technology emerged differently: Fascinating and enjoyable, yes, but as a framework only disguised as choice. You can pick your platform, pick your level of engagement. But not participating at all now carries its own exile: social, professional, even existential. Presence has become infrastructural.

Like ascribed identities, digital life entangles agency. We are not choosing to abandon the physical. We still love the sun on our skin, a good meal, a long shower. We still enjoy travel and sex and music and sleep.

Within the digital realm, choice does exist, but only inside parameters we didn't design. Sometimes there is no choice at all. Ever tried navigating an automated phone tree? "Press one for English." "I'm sorry, I didn't understand that. Goodbye."

We are intertwined. We hold our phones in hand, videoing, while attending a concert.

The interface is chosen, but the effects are not. What emerges is a physiological blend of reward and punishment.

In digital systems, what follows our choices is often built on inference. Platforms track our behavior, compare it to others, and begin to guess what we might want before we decide. The feedback loop reshapes our experience without asking us to confirm. It is not always coercive. But it is always predictive. Over time, we may forget where the choice ended and the suggestion began. That is, if the process is even visible to us at all.

We welcome the interface because of all it has to offer. The convenience. The connection. The power to extend ourselves. At times, the fun!

What we did not fully anticipate were the conditions that came bundled with it. Upon closer examination, *they don't remotely resemble distraction*. In fact, they're closer to hyper-attention. New, invasive thoughts and emotions occupy our daily existence.

Neil Postman once wrote that technology always has unforeseen consequences, and you do not get to choose only the good parts.

That's true here. Our agreement was mostly implicit. We accepted the benefits without being shown the full cost. We said "I do," without getting to know our new partner first.

We used to have only reputations. Now we have algorithms, too. **We were once whole by default. Now we must learn to be whole by design.**

SO, WHAT CHANGED?

It seems like the arrival of widespread use of the internet alarmed us. It was in development for decades, then suddenly it was here.

We'll examine the timeline more closely in a later chapter. The world's academic circles reacted with concern. There were many studies. Professors, psychologists, teachers and parents began warning us about the very valid risks of having an online presence.

Their message was clear: we should disengage from digital platforms.

Sherry Turkle is an MIT sociologist and foundational voice on digital presence, a true pioneer. She laid the framework for a lot of the conversations we've had as a society about the internet age.

Her belief was that "Too much online time can leave us less connected to ourselves and to each other."

Jenny Odell, a former Stanford professor, writer and artist, wrote *How to Do Nothing: Resisting the Attention Economy*. Her book was a New York Times best seller.

Odell's work on the attention economy argues for reconnecting with the physical world to "resist digital overwhelm".

Jaron Lanier, a computer scientist and VR pioneer, wrote a book called *Ten Arguments for Deleting Your Social Media Accounts Right Now*. He put it more bluntly, "Addiction gradually turns you into a zombie. Zombies don't have free will."

It's true that in some cases, the best option is to log off completely. Like during dinner. Or during class.

It's also true that the internet can be a dangerous place. And living a life where you never touch grass is obviously not healthy.

I'm not here to disagree. I'm here to *qualify*. All of that is accurate, but today things are more nuanced. Turkle wrote those words in 2011 and 2015. Odell expressed her views in 2019, and Lanier's book came out in 2018. A lot has changed since then.

Peripheral technology has increased Digital activity that doesn't involve screens is often referred to as *ambient intelligence* or *ubiquitous computing*. These terms describe technologies that operate seamlessly in the background, enabling interactions without the need for direct engagement with screens. Examples include voice-activated assistants like Amazon's Alexa or Google Assistant, smart home devices that adjust lighting or temperature automatically, and wearable technologies that monitor health metrics.

In 2019, the ambient intelligence market was valued at approximately $19.2 billion. By 2025, projections estimate the market will reach around $123.28 billion.

ChatGPT launched in late 2022. Artificial Intelligence (AI) in commercial automation didn't reach the point where it was marketable until around 2020, and back then it wasn't as reliable as it is today. As a result, it hadn't become widespread until more recently. Now, many of the products we buy were either manufactured or delivered to us (or both) using machine learning and generative AI in the process. Walmart and Lenovo are among the companies using this technology.

Activity involving actual screens has increased too. Access to public services like DMV appointments, unemployment benefits, visa processing, or healthcare portals, often require navigating clunky websites or apps. In many cases, taking the non-digital route often takes hours to accomplish the same thing that can be taken care of in minutes, with a few clicks. Other examples include boarding passes for airlines and self-service kiosks at airports, event tickets, mobile banking, QR code menus at restaurants, work-related activities, students submitting homework digitally, and self-checkout.

Even with the choices we do make, there are algorithms running in the background that we're not aware of, making decisions on our behalf.

Anyone with an investment portfolio, a savings account, 401(k), retirement account, stock holdings, or managed portfolio is being tracked, categorized, and acted upon by predictive systems designed to anticipate risk, behavior, and value. These decisions are made in real time and at scale, regardless of whether the investor is logged in.

Online video chats are on the rise as well, and have been particularly valuable to use in terms of time, travel costs, and accessibility.

Meetings for work, medical appointments, and online classes are just a few ways that we save substantial amounts of time and travel expense by simply meeting online instead.

Sometimes, alternative methods are available, but they result in slower service or being forced to ask for assistance, which is sometimes unavailable. In other instances, alternatives are not available at all.

All of that means that today, opting out entirely is an illusion. The digital world is an unavoidable part of life. Even if you don't own a smartphone and never touch a computer, you still have a digital presence.

Fortunately, as jarring as the onset of the digital age had been, it is still one of the greatest innovations in the history of humanity. It has transformed the way we generate knowledge, solve problems, build relationships, and expand what human systems are capable of. It has altered everything from medicine to space travel.

As the digital realm becomes ever more useful, as it continues to save lives and make new things possible, I believe a new view will come into focus. Online time will no longer be the enemy.

In actuality, the digital realm already is ambient and ubiquitous. It isn't solely harmful or useful. It's both, and everything in between.

It's where you check your bank balance and do other mundane tasks.

You work in the digital realm. In most cases that's true even if you work with your hands.

You play, you visit and connect there. You solve problems, do research, ask and answer questions.

Still, for all its brilliance, something about it does feel off. We can feel that same discomfort the scholars, experts, teachers, parents, and so many others do, and we should trust our instincts. The naysayers, those who blindly misuse the digital realm, will likely be the last to realize.

But to chalk it up to too much screen time or a lack of willpower has become an oversimplification. Up to now, our assumptions have been mostly based in emotion, fear even.

Upon further examination, the unease is actually structural. It comes from a mismatch between the human mind and the system surrounding it. It's time for us explore what's really happening, what exactly we are adapting to.

Early automobiles also faced a great deal of criticism when they first appeared. That transition from initial skepticism, to acceptance, then finally to integration is similar to what we're experiencing now in the digital age.

Cars and airplanes have revolutionized transportation. Yet they pollute, deplete us of fossil fuel resources, and can be unsafe.

Pharmaceuticals are similar. They save countless lives, but illicit drugs create addicts and kill people.

There is a Greek term, *pharmakon*. In his 1968 essay, *Plato's Pharmacy*, French philosopher, Jacques Derrida revived the term in his work. It describes this double-edged sword as 'both remedy and poison' (an indirect translation of the Greek word). Later, a second French philosopher, Bernard Stiegler extended Derrida's ideas into media theory, digital technology, and memory, particularly via his three-volume work *Technics and Time*.

Here, we'll apply Stiegler's theory of pharmakon to build a more nuanced view. The goal is to elevate the digital debate beyond binary thinking (harm vs. benefit).

It's not unusual at all for us to experience discomfort with things that are both new and groundbreaking. They never arrive with an explanation that satisfies us. That's the social cost for the majority of innovations.

Society's reaction has been both intellectual and visceral. In the following chapters, the assumption will be that we have expanded our view of the digital realm to mean ubiquitous. That screen time itself is not the problem, just like the car or the drug is not the problem. It's how it's used.

The impact has been discussed extensively, but there's one truth we've yet to fully grasp: unlike the car, which serves a single purpose (transportation), and is parked when no longer in use, the digital era brought more than new modes of communication or consumption that are always with us. It reshaped what it means to be present. It introduced a new kind of self.

CHAPTER TWO
My Social Amygdala

THRESHOLD MOMENTS

Here's what is different, and remarkable. Presence was once tied to action. A person moved, spoke, or appeared, and presence followed. In digital systems, the sequence is reversed. You are present *before* you arrive and participate.

Physically, when a person moves, speaks, or appears, their presence is observed. It doesn't even need to be in real time. The observer, and the awareness of presence, can come later.

Take, for example, a hiker who leaves a campsite. Hours pass. Another hiker walks up the same trail and encounters an area that looks like it has recently been cleared of brush and debris. In the clearing, there are ashes and half-burned logs where a campfire once was, and footprints. No one is there, but presence is obvious.

Metaphysically, the second hiker experienced existence of another presence.

In digital systems, the sequence reverses. Systems allocate space, prepare responses, and adjust conditions based on your *anticipated* presence.

The shift was subtle. At first, we trained the system. We gave it input, clicked, typed, and scrolled.

But at some point, the system began training itself *on us*. Behavior became *recursive*.

Recursivity
noun
/ri-ˈkər-sə-və-tē/

A self-reinforcing loop of interaction, interpretation and adaptation.

Recursive feedback loops back on itself and changes outcome. The function calls itself, then evolves based on the response. Each input refines future outputs, creating a self-reinforcing circle of interaction, interpretation, and adaptation.

Recursivity is already the defining architecture of nearly every major digital system today, from social platforms to search algorithms to smart assistants.

These systems process the input they receive, then they adjust based on it. They learn from behavior, then use that learning to shape what happens next, which then feeds new behavior. That loop is the norm, not the exception.

The digital realm is already deeply structured by it. Here, we'll examine the mechanics already at work.

We can also expect recursivity to define the trajectory of the digital age itself in the future. Examining it serves as our lens into the digital realm.

RECURSIVITY, TO HUMANS

Within a system, recursive feedback loops are simple, kind of boring, actually:

If > then (non-recursive, at this point):

If the user clicks the button, then show some content.

Recursivity enters:

Record how often and when the user clicks.

Use that pattern to change the timing, color, wording, or placement of the content next time.

Repeat, based on newly gathered behavior.

Over time, recursive systems optimize themselves, shaping not only their response until, eventually the entire context of interaction is permanently reshaped. This is how algorithms become "smart" and how platforms evolve in real-time with user data.

We see that as ever-changing content, and it keeps us captivated.

When the system began using your presence to decide what presence should look like, suddenly your attention was redefined. It was no longer something that altered the feed. It began to shape the algorithm behind the feed.

Because the digital realm is evolving because of your actions, your output has become future input. Since your behavior trains the model, and the model influences your behavior, you've moved beyond interaction.

Your "self" is baked into a system's causal structure, before you act, speak, appear, or are even inferred. We are presupposed.

That is pre-ontological embedding, where existence is presumed before it appears.

PRE-ONTOLOGICAL EMBEDDING

The term "ontology" was coined in 1613.

The concept was created by philosophers to help us understand that there are different categories of what we call reality. Simply put, it asks; **what exists, and in what way?**

The experts, of course, were theorizing during a period time long before there was a digital realm.

In the 1930s, German philosopher Martin Heidegger's work shifted ontology from what a thing is to how it shows up in our interaction with the world. At the time, his work was groundbreaking. A split from substance-essence metaphysics toward *functional* being.

After that, things were fairly status quo in the realm of ontology until the 1990s, when another philosopher, Gilles Deleuze, brought the concept of "the fragmented self" into our consciousness. His theories are foundational for this book.

Deleuze's theory brought identity into the digital age. He said, "You aren't one thing. You're many little pieces. Data, preferences, tags." In the modern world, especially online, we're often not seen as whole people. You might be a username, a purchase history, a voting record, a credit score. Those pieces can be separated, re-used, and interpreted without your knowledge.

Deleuze showed us that identity is no longer unified: it's divisible, sortable, and functional. He identified duality.

Just a decade or so later, a third philosopher, Benjamin H. Bratton brought into our consciousness the very different way systems see us, than we see ourselves or others. In the digital realm, the system knows what device you're on, what protocol you connect through, and what server or cloud you pass through to get to your online destination. To Bratton, digital identity had become a "network condition", not a personal trait. He made clear that online, you exist if, and only if, you're legible to the machine.

Their work redefined ontology. If I had been writing this in 1613, or even 1930, the proxy self would have failed to meet the criteria of traditional ontology. All the boxes would have been checked, leaving only one remaining; that it is a human-engineered construct. Depending on who you asked, the reasoning might have been: its existence and operation are inextricably linked to human design, intention, and infrastructure. So even though it is present in our lives, shapes perceptions, and meets all other ontological criteria, it would have still been considered a "dependent entity", reflecting human agency rather than qualifying as an "autonomous being."

Forgive me if I take just a quick second to (respectfully) call out the philosophers I admire so much. If you're in a science or tech-related field, this may make you smile with recognition. It appears there might have always been a bit of hypocrisy involved. At the same time as philosophers were busy arguing about whether or not the digital realm could be defined as an ontological presence, they were asserting that buildings, roads and airplanes did.

At the time of this writing, even Wikipedia presents an out-of-date view.

Many of those who didn't feel compelled to support Deleuze and Bratton in their theories changed their mind entirely when they considered just one thing: both had asserted that the digital realm passed the test of being ontologically present *before* the arrival of artificial intelligence (AI).

In around 2023, there was a notable inflection point in defining ontological being. The rise of sophisticated AI and ubiquitous personalization made it difficult to deny the existence of some kind of presence.

Traditional thinking saw intelligence as rules and logic. AI proved that messy, opaque systems (like neural networks) could outperform human logic, even when we can't explain how. It proved what we always knew, Intelligence, and existence itself, is something that doesn't need to be explained to be real.

If presence could no longer be adequately measured using traditional criteria, we needed to redefine how we once understood being.

In retrospect, the moment we began rewriting the terms for what counts as real is not a single event.

The era of recursive platforms emerged around 2009. We saw Facebook's News Feed optimization, Google's shift from static results to predictive/auto-complete/knowledge graph, the rise of YouTube's autoplay and algorithmic escalation, Siri, the first casual, system-facing AI assistant, Amazon's anticipatory shipping patents, and the birth of filter bubbles and system-shaped knowledge emerged. This is when the idea of "you" began to be built without your involvement, and real-world experiences began shaping around those digital versions.

At that point, most of us had already crossed the proxy line.

We'll look at that a few ways. First, we'll reconstruct ontology to encompass both physical and digital *presence*.

Then, we'll put it to the test with the concept of fidelity, and the capacity of a proxy identity to imprint itself on the system as a recursive *participant* in shaping system evolution.

That will be followed up by examining it in an epistemological sense; How do we know what we're seeing or experiencing is real?

We'll explore phenomenology; how is it experienced? Then, move on to pragmatism What are the consequences of its existence? Next, we'll study the sociological and cultural effects of the proxy condition. After that, we'll examine neurological evidence that supports it.

CHAPTER THREE
Ontological Presence

DEFINING PRESENCE

If we're discussing presence, the newer, expanded view of ontology is the logical place to start. Here, we'll use it as a benchmark for existence, the *what* and the *how*. We will explore the similarities and differences of classical metaphysics and the operational reality of system-mediated existence.

TIME ISN'T LOST, IT'S RESTRUCTURED

With books and television, time unfolds in sequence. You begin, you follow, and you finish. The experience is bounded by structure and expectation; you always know when you've exited.

Digital time, by contrast, has no defined entry or exit. Notifications ignore beginnings, and interrupt middles. Algorithms remove endings. The moment stretches, loops, refreshes, and reengages. What begins as a glance becomes a loop. There's no sign that you've left and there was never a clear moment you arrived.

Fig. 3:1 Original Realms of Ontology
Historically and in modern theory, this breaks into three foundational realms.

REALM (AXIS)	KEY PREMISE	MODE OF BEING
Substance & Essence	What is a thing?	Materiality, identity, coherence
Relational & Functional	What does a thing do or relate to?	Use, causality, affordance
Representational & Informational	How is a thing understood or modeled?	Symbol, data, simulation

John Suler's *Psychology of the Digital Age* identifies how psychological navigation through digital platforms allows users to assemble a self that is both continuous and legible to systems and others.

In physical life, norms emerge from habit and social pressure. In digital life, they emerge through systems design.

Now that you no longer have to show up to be active, systems can run a version of you without you. That means presence today isn't just about being remembered (legacy) or consciously participating. This is the point at which humans added that new layer to ontology, the new type of presence that is a system function, not a human act.

With that in mind, we take the work of the pioneering **ontological** philosophers, as well as that of Postman, Turkle, Zuboff, together with AI literature, and with their theories as a template, we explore this new, AI-driven state.

> **Ontological Presence**
> noun
> /ˌän-ˈtä-lə-ji-kəl ˈpre-zəns/
>
> The condition in which a self is recognized as real by a system because it causes action or effect. In the proxy condition, being is measured by existence, systemic interaction and consequence.

Ontology asks, *what does it mean for something to exist?* In classical terms, that meant:

Substance

Aristotle gave us this criterion: Is it a "thing"?

Essence

Plato asked: What makes it what it is?

Perception

Descartes, then Locke further clarified: Can it be known or sensed?

Coherence

Does it show up meaningfully in the world?

The original test of existence was: *Can it be known, encountered, or acted through?* Heidegger took it a step further.

In digital systems, we use different methods to express being encountered, experienced, or acted through:

Legibility

Can the system read it? (Aristotle: Is it a "thing"?)

In digital ontology, legibility is the precondition for potential being. In analogical terms: as Plato's Form is to soul, so is legibility to system: not yet acting, but awaiting instantiation. For Aristotle, substance is what everything else depends on. In digital systems, that substance is code. It's something that can be activated, referenced, and used. To a system, what it cannot parse does not exist.

Essence

What instantiates the identity? It must become a running agent, not just data: (Plato: What makes it what it is?)

In classical ontology, Heidegger's hammer exists most authentically in its use. In a proxy condition, essence is revealed only through execution. Instantiation means making something actually work, not merely simulating it. Plato's Forms are timeless and unchanging. Digital proxies are temporary and editable. Still, both serve as templates for creating instances. In that way, legibility becomes the system's way of knowing.

Fig. 3:2 Ontological Presence
A framework for understanding post-human presence.

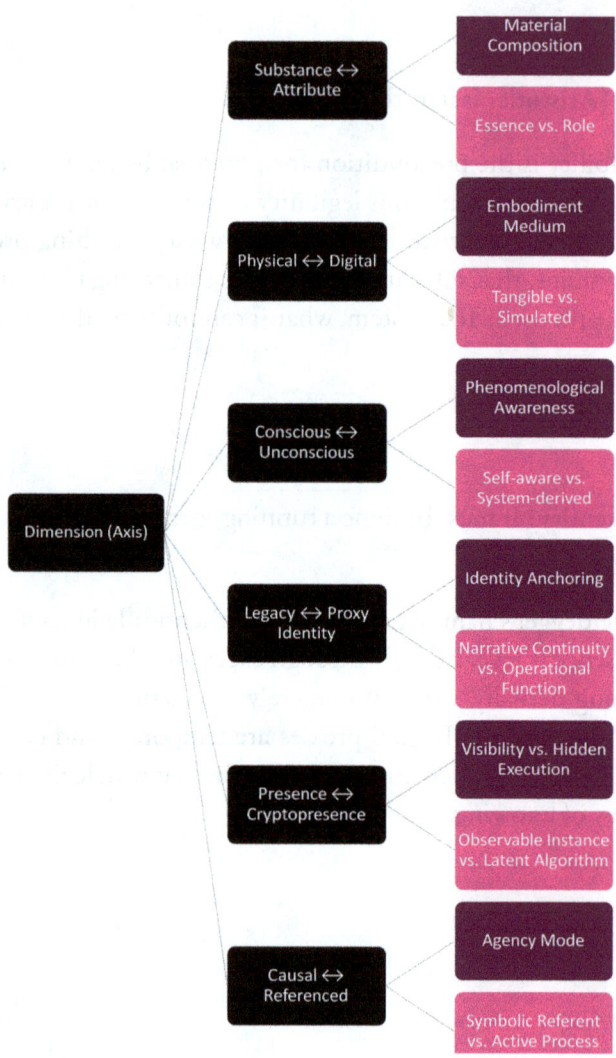

Perception

The identity must affect outcomes; it must be registered or responded to by the system. (Descartes, Locke: Can it be known or sensed?).

The identity must affect outcomes; it must be registered or responded to by the system. In other words, it must be perceptible within the system's logic.

For Descartes and Locke, this raises the question: Can it be known or sensed? In the proxy condition, perception is not just sensory, but systemic. It is defined by what the system can detect, interpret, and act upon.

The Proxy Condition
noun
/ˈpräk-sē kən-ˈdi-shən/

A metaphysical state in which the self is constituted across two incompatible systems (digital and physical, algorithmic and embodied) that do not share a unified frame for recognition.

Coherence

Coherence is implied across all three. The proxy becomes real only when it operates as part of the system's logic loop (Heidegger: Does it show up meaningfully in the world?)

Heidegger sees presence as more than just what we see or use. In a system-driven world, presence is revealed being visible and usable within the system.

Together, these four create the architecture of digital presence. Legibility makes you visible. Essence runs you. Perception proves you influence outcomes. Coherence confirms you're integrated. Without all four, you exist in the system, but not as a functioning identity.

CAUSAL AGENCY

The language will differ because the interpreter is now a system, but all the conditions must still be met. For causal agency to rise to the level of proxy presence, the system has to respond, and the identity must act as a cause.

Plato's essence was eternal form. Here, the eternal form exists as data (form) that is legible and actionable (essence and coherence) without your direct involvement (eternal).

Aristotle's substance was actuality. In this case, instantiation is execution. We described that as runnable or executable. Descartes' perception was human awareness, perception. Heidegger's coherence was tool-use. The tool is the app, the device, the algorithm, or the login. System coherence is being executable in context. The execution is the tool.

In classical ontology, something was considered real if it could be perceived or used meaningfully. In the proxy condition, the bar for qualifying as causal agency is higher:

It's not just seen, it does. It absorbs perception, extends coherence, and **becomes the operational validator of digital presence**. In proxy systems, causal agency isn't what you intend. It's what the system does because of you. Presence is proven by effect.

Some identities may be legible and even instantiated, but not yet causal. Others may be instantiated without full legibility, operating as fragments without formal recognition.

These liminal states form a zone of *'pre-proxies'*: forms that exist in potential, but do not yet function as operational entities. For example, a dormant Instagram account may still be seen and stored, but if it doesn't trigger recommendation logic, it remains a pre-proxy, or a shadow identity. If all conditions are met, an identity registers ontologically as a system-level presence.

THE UNSEEN CLASS

Not all identities meet the criteria for presence. Some remain suspended in potential. They are legible but dormant, or instantiated but unregistered.

These are pre-proxies. Recognized, but non-causal, stored, but non-reactive, seen, but not yet system-integrated,

They form a class of unseen entities beings within system ontology. Think of ghost forms that haunt logic but do not alter it.

Pre-proxies are the preconditions of digital being, just as unstruck matches are the preconditions of fire.

Fig. 3:3 Ontological Test of Presence in the Proxy Condition
An identity becomes system-operable only when all four conditions are met.

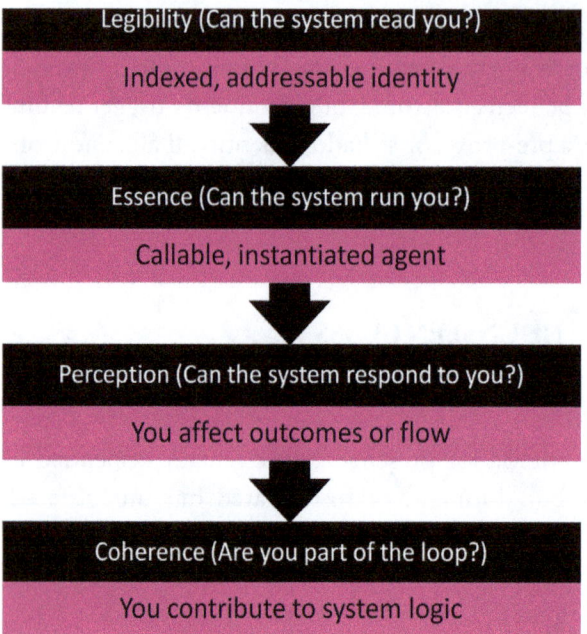

Together, these four conditions shift the question from "Are you online?" to "Are you operable, operated, responsive, and structurally embedded?" That's the real test of presence in the proxy condition, and in our case, all those conditions are true.

We can now observe, in both time and behavior, the moment the proxy condition emerged. Once it met the measurable criteria for existence, it ceased to be metaphor. We can validate that, for some time now, it has functioned as an ontological fact.

CHAPTER FOUR
A New Taxonomy of Fidelity

WHAT THE SYSTEM SEES, IT CAN SORT

So far, we've defined presence in digital systems as a presence, the proxy self.

Fidelity is the bridge between representation and identity. Here, the question becomes: does the proxy self represent you accurately?

Now, we'll explore the forms that representation takes.

Pre-Proxies

Pre-proxies are fragments. They are indexed but inert. These identities are known to the system but not called upon. Think of them as preconditions of presence: the structure exists, but it has not become operative.

A stored identity that never logs in would be an example. Let's say a bank you used to have an account with was acquired by another bank, and the two companies merged. You no longer bank there. But somehow, maybe erroneously, your closed account was imported into the new bank's system. It's there, but no one has ever accessed it.

A dormant user account would also be such an inoperative fragment, as would any metadata that never triggers any outcome.

The Eleatic Principle states: if it has no effect, it does not exist.

For all its controversy in metaphysics, in digital systems, where existence is determined by execution, the principle is relevant.

Fidelity vs. Legibility
distinction
/fə-ˈde-lə-tē/ vs. /ˈle-jə-bə-lə-tē/

Fidelity is internal truth; legibility is external readability. The two are not aligned by default.

In the proxy condition, you can be completely coherent to yourself

---

Something doesn't become real until it's used and causes the system to behave differently. You can be in the system and still not be a part of it. Dormant accounts. Forgotten clicks. Broken hyperlinks. Cached fragments. Until something is acted on or causes action, it remains outside the perimeter of causal presence.

This is the cut. A proxy identity isn't just stored. It shapes behavior. Only then does it exist in the system's world.

A record may be readable and referenced in summaries or reports (e.g. the number of accounts the new bank has), but if it does not influence system behavior, if it is not called, executed, or causes change, it remains a pre-proxy. Presence is measured not by inclusion, but by consequence.

Proxies

Now, let's say that same, inactive bank account is included in a report that automatically runs monthly. At that point, it's still a pre-proxy. You, represented by your old account, are still not present in the operational sense.

Let's imagine, however, that the bank's managers have put a flag in the system to lower interest rates once the number of customers exceeds 50,000. Your dormant account just happens to be account 50,001, and there are no more. 50,0001 accounts, in total.

Now, your account has triggered a system behavior. That means it has crossed the threshold into causality. You haven't acted, but the system has, because of your presence.

Your account is now a proxy. Dormancy ended the moment consequence began.

A proxy is a system-operable identity. It exists in execution, not in name only. It is legible, instantiated, and affects outcomes. These are the working selves of digital life.

To qualify as a proxy, an identity needs to be legible, can run, can affect outcomes, and is included in system logic.

Proxies shape experience within the system. They don't just appear; they operate. Most people now function as proxies, though they may not be aware of it.

Imprint Identity (Agents of Fidelity)

Today, most proxies advance. They exceed operational presence and begin to alter the structure they exist within. These are imprint identities, or agents of fidelity. When the system is changed as a result of them, the loop becomes recursive.

In our bank example, where we left off, your dormant account, number 50,001, had triggered a flag to lower interest rates for all customers. Let's imagine that activity triggered another flag (even if it was in the same query) to ignore inactive accounts, and your account being excluded was the cause for interest rates to remain the same. Your account has revised the rule itself. The system now incorporates your footprint into its behavior.

Fig. 4:1 Pre-Proxy/Legacy Presence vs. Proxy Presence Achieved

Historically and in modern theory, this breaks into three foundational realms.

WHO?	PROXY PRESENCE?	WHY?
All consumers, even those offline	✓	Automation operates in the background, altering commerce, cost of goods, and supply chain.
Everyday users with detailed behavioral profiles (Netflix, TikTok, Spotify)	✓	Their presence alters recommendation engines in real time based on prediction loops.
Anyone who triggers system decisions in adaptive systems (e.g., fraud detection, credit scoring)	✓	The model doesn't simulate them for interface, but their identity causes state changes. Still a form of proxy presence.
Individuals whose likeness appears in real-time generative outputs (e.g., face swap filters)	✓	If their digital form shapes outputs across interactions, they are causal, even without awareness.
Authors who've trained models to answer questions "in their voice"	✓	Their model is legible, executable, and alters outputs. The agent speaks on their behalf.
AI influencers (e.g., vocal clones, deepfake avatars who interact with audiences)	✓	The system runs them directly, engages users through them, and modifies itself based on those interactions.
Someone mentioned in a book or academic citation	✗	They're referenced but not encoded in a system. No legibility or instantiation. Legacy presence only.
A person whose face is in a training dataset, but can't be prompted, queried, or mapped to a profile	✗	The trace is legible in structure, but not instantiated or callable. They are in the system, but not of it.
A user whose data are stored but never acted on (e.g., dormant accounts)	✗	Legible, maybe instantiable, but no system state is changed by them.
People in analog media archives (VHS, print, film)	✗	Machine-invisible. May be remembered or mythologized, but have no system presence.

Fig. 4:2 SQL Queries Illustrating Bank Example
Two different queries that, in this instance, return the same results.

```
if COUNT > 50000 then reduce_rate
if COUNT(active_accounts) > 50000 then reduce_rate
```

In the first bank example, your account was filtered out before the system made any changes. The order of logic determines whether presence becomes consequence. Since it was excluded before the system responded, it remains latent. But if its inclusion causes a result, it crosses the threshold into imprint identity.

Even if that result is invisible to us. It usually is, in every one of these instances:

Anytime you're on social media, your experience is recursive. What you view and like will play a role in what is shown to others.

Most popular games rely on recursive techniques. If you're winning too often, they'll make the play more challenging or your opponents more skillful. Research shows, if you feel unchallenged, you will lose interest quickly.

Educational platforms like Duolingo rely on recursive techniques too. If you, and many others, consistently have difficulty with a certain question, the system will flag it as a "bad" question, and replace it with another. At that point, users have shaped it.

The examples are too numerous to mention; your behavior reshaping a recommendation engine, your role in altering predictive text, and your patterns training a model that persists beyond your interaction. These are all instances in which you cross the proxy line and enter fidelity, or presence.

YOU RECURSIVELY SHAPE SYSTEM BEHAVIOR

Where coherence makes you a part of the system's loop, fidelity makes you part of its memory and future logic. It is the point where presence evolves into persistence and eventually agency-with-continuity. You've moved beyond the loop. You're now altering it, shaping it, bending it.

In classical ontology, there's no perfect analogy, but Heidegger's concept of thrownness (Geworfenheit), the idea that existence is shaped by being "thrown into" a world with history, comes close.

In the digital proxy condition, fidelity expresses a kind of Heidegger's thrownness in reverse: the proxy changes the world it's thrown into. Fidelity asks:

"Does your presence alter the system's structure, behavior, or logic over time?"

> **Fidelity**
> noun
> /fə-ˈde-lə-tē/
>
> The persistence of presence across time and systems. A proxy gains fidelity when it is recognized repeatedly by the system in ways that preserve or evolve identity. Fidelity marks the shift from momentary input to structural memory.

If the answer is yes, then you rise to a new level above being perceived or coherent. You are remembered, referenced, and re-used. You're not just data in the system. You become part of its narrative logic.

But how, and why, does this rise to a level above mere data in the system?

To answer that question, we need to distinguish between passive inclusion and recursive operational significance.

Data can be stored, filtered, concatenated, and joined indefinitely. But that doesn't make it operative. Presence emerges when the data ceases to be about something and begins to act as a reference point for system behavior.

One might ask, isn't the data joined, concatenated, filtered? Doesn't it get analyzed as one big datastream? Aren't there instances where the system is agnostic to whether it is really one person?

Absolutely. It often is. But narrative logic goes beyond knowing who you are. It makes the assumption that you matter structurally, that you not only exist, but are factored in decisions the system will make on your behalf.

Where coherence placed you inside a loop you don't see, fidelity places you above it. You begin shaping what the loop becomes.

THE LAYERS OF PRESENCE

Presence in the proxy condition is layered. Each layer deepens system entanglement. The following captures those layers:

The system prepares for your arrival (prehension). The system can read you (legibility). The system can instantiate you (essence).

The system can be affected by you (perception). The system responds, it includes you in its logic (coherence). The system evolves because of you (fidelity).

As you scan the taxonomy on the next page, consider this:

If the system behaves differently because of you, you were present. Even if you never touched a screen. Attention could be as simple as a login. Binary and transactional. You cross the proxy line when your existence has a structural effect, when it alters system logic. Put simply, if you're part of how the system thinks, if you shape it, that's fidelity.

To take it a step further, when the system begins to update itself around your influence and its future conditions are structured by your past presence, you become more than operative. You become an imprint identity.

Imprint identities complete the proxy condition. You've now caused system evolution to evolve beyond your past behavior.

In traditional terms, this would be myth, legacy, infrastructure. Here, it's system memory with consequence. These agents of fidelity do not just participate in logic. They become part of how logic writes itself.

Fig. 4:3 Layers of Presence in the Proxy Condition
From anticipation to recursion: the six system-level thresholds that define digital being.

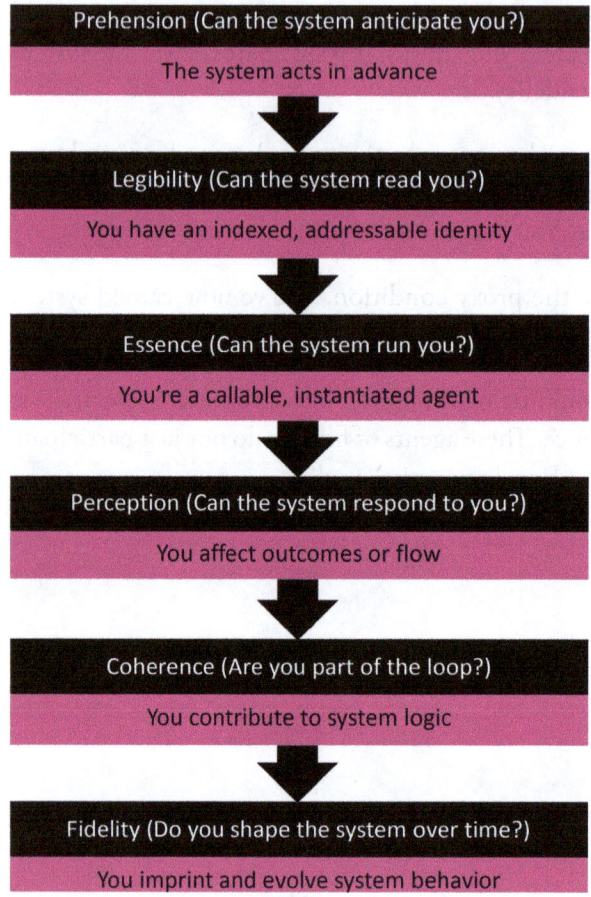

ONTOLOGY & FIDELITY

To sum things up, fidelity is what happens when presence becomes persistence. You are no longer just inside the loop. Instead, you're shaping what the loop becomes. In classical terms, this is Heidegger's thrownness in *reverse*: the proxy changes the world it is thrown into. The question fidelity asks is simple: Did your presence change the rules? If yes, your identity is now embedded in the system's architecture, not just recognized by it.

Even if the system doesn't understand you as you, it behaves as though your identity is causally coherent, across time, across contexts. That *as if* is the crucible of proxy presence.

In this framework:

Ontology

Being is what the system can act through. If the system can do something because of you, you *are*.

Fidelity

You're a presence when the system remembers you. This captures the shift from presence as visibility to presence as structural trace. You're not just known, but reused.

You are not present because you act. You are present because you're here, **and** your existence modifies the system that surrounds you.

That is what counts as real now.

CHAPTER FIVE
Epistemology

If presence can be real without awareness, can truth be true without anyone knowing it?

Ontology asks whether something is. Epistemology asks: how do we know that it is?

So, we ask; can what is known in a system count as knowledge for us? The challenge? How do you confirm a presence that is functionally real, but not physically observed?

In the digital realm, evidence is internal. Everything exists within an electronic system. It permeates our lives so much that it's hard to believe all we really have to show for it is a lot of hardware, and bytes being transferred to that hardware. Is knowledge still knowledge when it's held by a system, inferred and acted on in advance of human awareness?

That is the epistemological fault line of the proxy condition. Let's break it down. Epistemology has three key facets: truth, belief, and justification.

Truth

To be epistemologically valid, something must be true. In a digital environment where functions are called, then executed, that process is a form of truth. Did this happen? If yes, then a consequence resulted.

In the physical world, it's not uncommon for people to perceive truth as something that "comes out" after the fact.

An example: a man is sitting on his couch on a Saturday morning. Someone he recently matched with on Bumble texts: "Let's meet Tuesday at 7:00."

She's sincere, but uncertain. The truth is, she wants to see how the conversations between the two of them unfold between now and Tuesday. Her intent is to be there.

He enters the address and the time in his phone. He works out on Monday after work instead of Tuesday, so he'll be free. He wears something to work on Tuesday that he'll be comfortable meeting her in. An hour before, the notification pops up on his phone. He arrives at the coffee house at 6:55.

That is similar to how truth functions in digital systems. The initial text initiated a state change. Whether she arrived or not, her message produced a causal sequence of events. The message's truth shifts from her intent to the consequences it sets in motion.

In the physical world, we tend to assume that she told the truth, only if she shows up. A closer look tells us that logic is invalid in both the physical and the digital realm. It doesn't mean she didn't tell the truth at the time.

We tend to look at her arrival as the *validation* of the existence of epistemological truth. But what if her car broke down on her way there? That doesn't mean she lied.

That example shows us how systems look at truth. It is evidenced through action. It is validated by effect. It is communicated in advance, then proven through behavior. In this framework, the conditions were met, the response was exactly what the pre-calculated conditions said it would be.

To a system, truth is not what it reflects, but what it triggers.

Belief

Here, we pose what I believe is one of the most metaphysical questions that exists anywhere in the genre of the effects of the digital age upon society"

What is belief when it no longer requires a believer?

We live in a state where the order of enlightenment can work two ways. Belief can be something you hold, a conviction or trust that something is true. Or, it can exist in reverse. You don't scroll because you believe want to. You believe you want to because the system has already built the world around the prediction of what you will want.

In reality, belief has never been limited to conscious thought or singular emotion. It has always been a force. It acts. It causes things to happen. You could always hold a belief that you didn't realize you had, until the circumstances around you caused it to surface.

In the digital environment, this is how belief always works. You're not choosing what you see. You're seeing what was already structured around what the system assumes you'll do. That assumption becomes your environment. And your reaction prompts the system's reinforcement of your belief.

In this way, your own belief escapes your mind and becomes part of the infrastructure. It is stored until you are present, then it enacts your belief on your behalf. It operates across time and systems, guiding what's shown, what's filtered, what's suppressed, and what's offered again. And if it works, it persists.

So when we talk about belief in the proxy condition, we're not talking about trust or doubt. We're talking about causal assumption.

Belief is a background condition of digital life. It shapes the world you enter to align with the beliefs it assumes you hold.

Justification

If you ask someone knowledgeable about classical epistemology, they won't get more than a sentence or two into their explanation before the word "justification" is mentioned. It is the epistemological cornerstone. You know something because you can justify it. You can explain why it's true.

In a machine-learning context, justification is not rational but recursive. The system justifies an inference by its performance, not its logic. You were shown this ad because people like you clicked it. If you see the ad, it was presented to you, its function validates it. Think of it as a retroactive justification.

Whether it's engagement, a purchase or the liking of a post, if a prediction leads to an action, and that action achieves the target outcome, then it becomes real. Knowledge becomes a series of conditional actions: if x, then show y. At that point, there is no further need for explanation. You just experienced something.

PROXY EPISTEMOLOGY

This is what we are left with: an epistemology not of knowledge, but of function. Not of belief, but of outcome.

In the proxy condition, the question is not: is it true? The question is: does the system act as if it is?

Systems build around those assumptions. So do we.

You check your feed to see what matters. You Google a symptom to see what you should worry about. You swipe to find someone worth dating. You type in a prompt, hoping to get a response that proves the system gets you.

The system acts first. You respond.

And if you respond consistently, your belief aligns with the system's belief proxy. You've outsourced your own epistemology. Not just how you know, but what counts as knowable.

In the next chapter, we ask: how do we experience this? What does it feel like to live inside a system that knows you before you speak?

CHAPTER SIX
Phenomenology

If epistemology deals with what can be known, phenomenology deals with how experience appears to us.

Digitally, the nature of experience itself is shaped before it reaches your awareness. Experience has always behaved that way, and continues to, every hour of every day. It's personal. Unique to us.

Say a father takes his child to the park to play. The father's reality is that he did that, as the child's father. The child's reality is that he was taken to the park to play.

In that sense, we always meet reality wherever we are. Since the digital world has always offered an experience, even early browsing had a phenomenological presence.

In 2007, a person scrolling through Facebook for the first time could describe what that moment felt like. They might recall the novelty of seeing friends' lives appear in a continuous feed. They might remember the way their attention moved from post to post, or how their emotions shifted while engaging with photos or comments. That experience was phenomenological. It didn't require feedback from the system. It required presence, attention, and the lived texture of the moment.

The arrival of recursion changed the stakes.

The park doesn't create a lower play structure in advance because the child had difficulty reaching the top of the one that's there.

Recursion tailors phenomenology to us.

How experience appears to us is how it appears to us, but also how it has appeared to us before.

Phenomenology describes what it feels like to live inside a sequence of perception.

In systems, what you encounter is what the system inferred you were ready to see. It was there because you would respond. And when you do respond, the system incorporates that into what it prepares next.

Fig. 6:1 Layers of Phenomenology in the Proxy Condition
The flow from presentation to reiteration reflects the phenomenological cycle in system-mediated environments. Presentation, reception and response alone are enough to qualify as conditions of phenomenology.

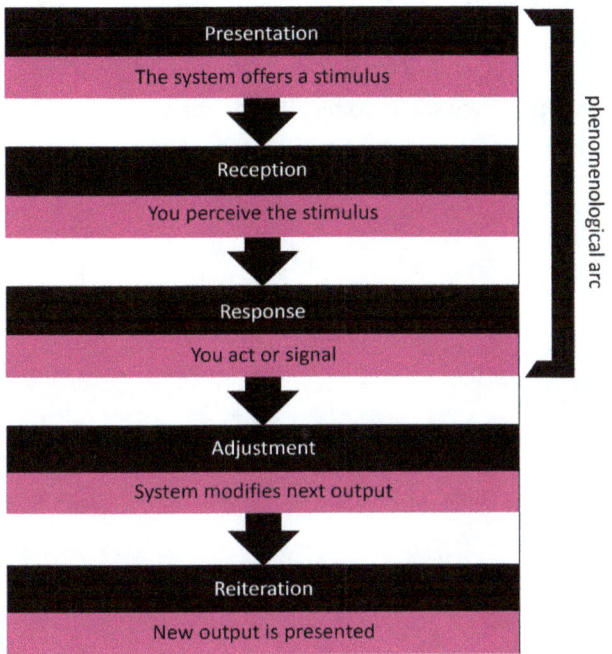

When a feed knows what you will like, it becomes a kind of mirror. But not a reflective mirror. A generative one that reflects back to you what you are expected to be. And it gives you that version in fragments. Each fragment is phenomenologically convincing. It feels real. It carries weight. It commands attention.

But the self who responds is often partial. You might not have chosen that version of yourself. You might not even recognize it.

THE PROXY CONDITION

You find yourself looking at clips of Brussels Griffons in your feed and you wonder how you got there, or who thought that would be a good idea.

But you'll react in the way that resembles your current mood. The more you do, the more it becomes your current mood. You continue to interact, and that version of you becomes the one the system reinforces.

It is at this point where the experience starts to feel like duality.

CHAPTER SEVEN

Pragmatism

Up to now, we've interwoven practical explanations in with concepts that are esoteric. Pragmatism, as the name suggests, is more straightforward.

At a high level, the digital realm is about as pragmatic as things get. Input produces output. It is pragmatic beyond human capability. What something means is what it does.

From the digital realm's humble beginnings, this has been true. A hyperlink meant redirection because it redirected. A forum meant discussion because people discussed.

Every element derived its meaning from the functional outcomes it produced. Pragmatism was quietly baked into the infrastructure from the beginning. In this light, the internet didn't just host pragmatism, it enacted it.

What if meaning was never spoken, only demonstrated? What if everything we know online has always meant what it does?

It does.

It actually can't behave any differently. In the proxy condition, meaning is not descriptive. It's operational. A profile doesn't describe who you are. It triggers actions. It tells the system what to show next.

A click doesn't signal interest. It updates the logic. A like doesn't mean you enjoyed something. It becomes an input. In digital environments, nothing is symbolic unless it causes an outcome. The system doesn't assign meaning based on appearance. It assigns meaning based on use.

This isn't a glitch or a byproduct. It is the structure. Interfaces may appear abstract, but the logic is exact. The more you interact, the more the system refines what your actions mean. Meaning isn't declared. It's detected.

That is pragmatism: what something means is what it does.

CHAPTER EIGHT
Foundational Traits

MEETING THE STANDARD FOR CULTURAL PERMANENCE

We move now into the sociological presence the digital world has formed among us.

Plato believed that every beautiful thing in the physical world is not Beauty itself, but merely an imperfect copy or instance of something higher: the *Form of Beauty*. If an artist saw a beautiful flower and painted that flower, the painting would be beautiful because it reflects the form (the beauty of the flower). But both the flower and the painting are limited, material, and perishable. Beauty will always be beauty, when the flower and the painting no longer exist.

Plato would have taught that the form itself exists, in a non-physical, eternal realm. It is unchanging and universal. It is *foundational*.

Plato defined essence not by how long something has existed in the material world, but by whether it reflects a timeless structure or principle that defines its nature.

Historically speaking, if the evolution of planet Earth were condensed into a single minute, modern humans would exist for less than a second. They would appear around the final 0.002 seconds. That puts the onset of the digital age approximately 0.0000004 seconds before the one-minute mark. So how can we be sure, with such a relatively short history, that it qualifies?

Essence, in this context, doesn't mean age. In the social sciences, permanence is not measured by time alone. Time is just one of several qualifying factors. Plato, and modern experts across disciplines, look at whether something shapes behavior, reinforces systems, and persists across change.

Foundational traits, as they relate to society, have many names. A sociologist might call them social structures (Durkheim) or cultural norms (Parsons). A psychologist would likely refer to them as heuristics (Tversky and Kahneman) or cognitive schema (Piaget). A philosopher might describe them as ideological frameworks (Marx), ontological commitments (Heidegger), habitus (Bourdieu), preconditions of experience (Kant), or first principles (Aristotle).

Regardless of terminology, experts agree, foundational traits must meet several core criteria:

Pervasive

The trait must appear across groups, cultures, and contexts.

The existence of a digital entity as part of everyday life is widespread across demographics. The middle class and wealthy have been entrenched for quite some time. As access to technology increases, this duality is spreading even to the poor, particularly among the young, who feel social pressure to maintain an online presence.

Similarly, IQ and traditional measures of intelligence don't seem to play a role. The highly educated, the barely literate, and everyone in between are all drawn into dual presence. The system does not reward thoughtfulness or insight. It rewards availability.

The same is true of age. You may have seen babies in strollers or sitting in restaurants, holding phones and watching cartoons. I was at a friend's house recently, and her adorable six-year-old daughter was carrying an iPad around, FaceTiming a classmate. A 7-year-old can manage a Roblox storefront.

My biggest demographic on LinkedIn is middle-aged attorneys. They post enthusiastically and often.

Many memes exist about grandparents being overly active or even intrusive on Facebook, often sharing excessive amounts of information. Whether or not that stereotype holds true, boomers are actively on social media, just like the rest of us. A retiree can use biometric login to manage their pension fund or use a health monitoring app.

According to 2024 estimates, about 66% to 67% of the global population is connected to the internet today in some form.

Roughly 5.4 billion people have some type of internet access. About 92% of the world's population owns a mobile phone, and around 76% own a smartphone specifically. Social media usage is estimated at around 62% of the global population.

In other words, predictably, the proxy condition will become even more widespread.

Enduring

They have to persist over time and resist superficial change.

Foundational traits can't be temporary or easily replaced. They have to remain stable even as other parts of the system change. Surface tools may evolve, platforms rise and fall, interfaces shift, but the underlying trait continues to shape behavior. It adapts, but it does not vanish.

Systemic

They are not isolated or accidental. They are evident in different parts of the culture, often in repeating or reinforcing patterns. It would take a major disruption to remove or change them, and without them, the culture would function differently.

In our lives today, tech is self-reinforcing because each act of participation generates the conditions for more. A single post leads to replies. A search prompts suggestions. Even a brief scroll recalibrates what the system will show you next. What begins as interaction quickly becomes a feedback loop. Your activity teaches the system how to keep you engaged, and that engagement creates new expectations for presence.

It's structurally embedded because opting out is more than just inconvenient. It is nearly incompatible with modern life. Job applications, school portals, medical records, and even basic social plans often require digital interaction. Without our explicit knowledge, dual presence is built into the platforms themselves. You are not just online. You are on display. You are archived, tagged, indexed, predicted, and rendered in fragments. The systems that do this are not waiting for your permission. They run you in the background whether you show up or not.

The proxy presence is not confined to a single culture either. It has spread across nearly every society technology has reached, adapting itself to different customs, languages, and traditions. Wherever connection is possible, the appeal of maintaining a digital presence follows. I still keep in touch with someone I met in Ethiopia years ago, through social media.

Catalytic

The trait is evident in large-scale behaviors, norms, or identities. It shapes society.

Experts across disciplines increasingly argue that technology has become a foundational trait of modern society. While they may not always use that exact term, there is a consensus that it meets the criteria.

A SOCIOLOGICAL PHENOMENON

We can all agree, it would be absurd to try to guess how long it will take the human race to stop posting, opining, reacting, and garnering attention. The answer is, nearly 100% likely, a resounding "never". We're social creatures, ego-driven souls. In The Power of Now, Eckhart Tolle wrote, "The ego tends to equate *having* with *being*: I have, therefore I am. And the more I have, the more I am."

Our eternal appetite for this type of interaction intersects with humanity in a way that the old media did, albeit in a more primitive fashion. When compared with what exists today, old media was incapable of satisfying the most critical point of all; *the inclusion of us in the process.*

Old media offered observation. Digital life invites participation. That shift is not simply technological. It does not simply shape behavior. It has become a second interface of the self.

Today, the second, ever-evolving, "you" consists of fragments of you. Over time, the picture will become more complete. Either way, it is markedly different from the persona others see when they meet us. It's structurally a second, living, interactive self.

You might ask; *if the digital self is algorithmically rewarded for consistency, visibility, and relatability, is it really "you" anymore? Or is it an adaptation? Is our second self chosen, or is it a part of someone's system?*

I get it. Driving down a road doesn't make you the traffic engineer.

But the way you drive still reshapes the flow. Participation doesn't always mean authorship.

Any login credentials, your credit score, your smartphone metadata, streaming services like Netflix, or a work ID badge are just a few examples. They are constructed by your behavior or role, but you don't directly author them. They alter something, personalize it.

Each of these creates feedback loops where interpretation becomes influence, and influence becomes self-reinforcement. It narrows choice and becomes an environment unique to you.

Yes, you choose what to post and interact with, but not how it's weighted, how it travels, or how it gets interpreted in the system's language. You feel like you're interacting, but behind the scenes your input is being processed. It enters a realm governed by logics that weren't made for you, but *around* you.

When presence becomes conditional, when silence becomes legible, and when your profile adapts to rules you didn't write, something larger is happening. What we're dealing with is no longer just identity. This is the proxy condition.

Some might say: this isn't new. Cause and consequence have always been around.

This is where it differs. Say that I plant a seed, then leave, and a decade later a tree has grown from the seed. It grows so big and tall that it cracks the foundation of a house next door. Have I not left a presence behind? Didn't my action persist and alter the structure of something I never touched again? That is presence, they'd say. Consequence. Agency, even.

But a tree doesn't act in your name. It doesn't register anywhere as you. It grows because of you, not *as* you. When you plant a seed and walk away, you do not remain. Only the object of your action remains. It is evidence of your past presence, not a continuation of it. The tree's growth follows biological law. It doesn't reference other trees for context or adjust itself to reflect who you were. That's a causal effect. But it doesn't then cause the house to rebuild itself differently next time because of that damage. There is no recursion.

In the physical world, presence happens in space. You arrive, you act, and eventually you leave. What remains is what was touched, said, or remembered. The effect stays with the environment. It doesn't adapt in response to you. In the digital realm, presence happens through logic. It is parsed, triggered, and looped. Even when you're silent, your proxy remains operable. The system still registers you. The interaction continues, whether or not you return. The room forgets. The system doesn't.

The digital self is legible. It affects outcomes and is referenced recursively in system logic. You leave something that keeps acting, and keeps being acted upon. It continues as you. It replies, it recommends, and shapes results in systems that interpret it as your voice.

To sum it up in Bourdieu's terms, the proxy presence constitutes a new 'field'. It is a structured social space with its own logic of participation, and generates a unique form of symbolic capital.

Digital presence also now functions as a 'social fact' in the Durkheimian sense. It is an external condition that shapes behavior regardless of personal belief.

All of this is evidence that the proxy condition satisfies the sociological definition of a presence.

The seed causes. The proxy continues. You're part of a referential system.

The tree just grows. The proxy *adapts*.

CHAPTER NINE
Your Brain Has Entered the Chat

MOVING THE SAILS TO CATCH THE BREEZE

Next up, we move away from the philosophical and the sociological implications. Here, we study the human brain, which was not wired for the type of input it is receiving, but is nonetheless the primary physical participant in the digital world.

Recent studies in cognitive neuroscience, behavioral psychology, and media theory are beginning to confirm what many of us have already felt. Evidence is emerging to show that our brains are adapting.

For example, in the *Handbook of Research on New Literacies*, Kimberly A. Lawless and P. G. Schrader analyzed users' web navigation as syntactically meaningful behavior, showing that even digital link trails reflect intentional movement akin to real-world pathways.

Across academic disciplines, patterns point to something measurable; real neurocognitive responses tied to how the proxy self is processed, stored, and rewarded at the level of the brain. The following studies offer early confirmation that this condition is not just conceptual. It has observable cognitive and behavioral effects.

NEUROCOGNITIVE EVIDENCE

Neuroscientific research suggests that two key brain systems play complementary roles in how we interact with digital environments. The findings show that we react to them in the same way we react in the physical realm.

The first is the ventral striatum. Think of it as your internal rewards calculator. It tells your brain: "That was good, do it again."

A 2022 study using simultaneous EEG and fMRI found strong ventral striatum activation when participants were evaluated through digital profiles. This confirms that digital interactions trigger real neurological responses, especially around perceived approval.

A 2016 study showed that teens viewing Instagram posts with more "likes" showed greater ventral striatum activity, correlating with increased desire to engage with those posts.

In 2013, it was determined that more frequent Facebook use was linked to greater nucleus accumbens (NAc) activation in response to self-related social reward. NAc is part of the ventral striatum.

The second area of the brain is our Default Mode Network (DMN).

In the human brain, the act of self-reflection takes place there. The DMN has a role in our memory, self-concept, and emotional processing. This is the part of our brain that is largely responsible for how we perceive and evaluate ourselves.

Think of the DMN as your internal narrative network. It tells your brain: "Who am I? What happened before? What might happen tomorrow?"

A 2020 review published in Neuroscience and Biobehavioral Reviews found that the DMN also lights up during imagined social contexts. This suggests that our digital self-presentations are processed as real extensions of self, not just hypothetical ones.

Of course, there are other parts of the brain involved; the Salience Network, Executive Control Network (ECN), the Amygdala and the Prefrontal Cortex (PFC). The reason experts refer to these two as "primary" is because the other regions as modulators, not leads. In other words, they shape, regulate, or coordinate these core processes, but don't directly drive the experience.

Think of the ventral striatum as the spark, and the DMN as the story.

When we ask "What if you've been trying to live once while existing twice?" That's the DMN talking (narrative confusion, self-perception conflict).

When we say "You stayed up late hoping for more views on your reel," we're talking about the ventral striatum (the dopamine loop driving behavior).

These two areas interact, creating a dual consciousness: one rooted in physiological reward and the other in existential interpretation. Together, they describe both the behavioral pull and the existential weight of digital life.

Note that dual consciousness, as used here, refers to a split between physical brain processes and self-perception in digital interaction, not a dissociative or pathological state.

FINDINGS IN MEDIA PSYCHOLOGY

A 2022 study in Frontiers in Psychology found that teens who carefully managed how they presented themselves online were more likely to compare themselves to others and felt less emotionally stable. This suggests the second self affects not just how we are seen, but how we feel.

On a more positive note, a large-scale 2020 study published in Nature Communications found that individuals who expressed themselves authentically on social media reported higher levels of life satisfaction. The findings suggest that online identity has direct psychological effects and that alignment between physical and digital self-presentation contributes to well-being.

FINDINGS IN BEHAVIORAL PSYCHOLOGY

In 2019, researchers published findings showing that time spent immersed in digital platforms can increase feelings of presence and character identification. Participants reported that their digital personas felt integrated with their sense of self. This supports the idea that the proxy is not just an interface. It becomes a lived identity over time.

A 2022 article in Social and Personality Psychology Compass revealed a fundamental shift:

Identity is no longer shaped solely by real-world experience. Digital spaces now function as full environments for identity development.

Who we are is co-constructed through ongoing interaction, feedback, and self-curation, both from our physical existence and our digital one.

ZEROES AND ONES

Later chapters will explore how this condition reshapes authorship, memory, autonomy, and morality. For now, let's sum up how we've defined presence from philosophical, neurological, systemic, and behavioral perspectives. The following table offers a unified summary of these domains, and how they align across the physical self and its proxy.

Fig. 9:1 The Proxy Line
Where identity begins to operate beyond the self, and qualifies as present ontologically, neurologically, systemically, and behaviorally. The center line represents the proxy line.

PHYSICAL SELF	DIGITAL PROXY
Volitional action: You choose what to do	System-executed behavior: The system acts on your data
Conscious presence: You are aware of what's happening	Asynchronous visibility: You're visible online even when you're offline
Contextual interpretation: People infer meaning from facial cues, speech, setting	Algorithmic interpretation: Algorithms interpret you based on behavior
Anchored in time and place: You exist in a single moment and location	Persistent, ambient, and cached: You exist and move across platforms and time
Controlled authorship: You decide what to say or share	Recomposed from metadata, code: Your activity is reshaped and reused

Looking at the bigger picture, systems do not define what a person is, only who counts as present in the digital realm.

To qualify as present in the proxy condition, you must be both operable and operat*ing*. The system needs to be able to both read and run you, to actively use you in its logic. Almost no one who ceased to have an online presence after 2010 would fully meet the criteria of causal agency.

I think it's very important to point out, these threshold conditions do not imply ethical consent, emotional reality, or human value. They describe structure, not meaning or worth. They trace the process of presence that occurs when an identity functions as an entity within a system.

The same is true for the evolving nature of digital personhood in law (e.g., likeness rights, AI avatars). This work does not resolve the ethical, legal, or political consequences of the proxy condition. It offers no prescriptions, no policy, and no moral decree. Its aim is purely metaphysical: to define the altered architecture of presence in a world where systems remember faster than we do, and where identity is instantiated before it is authored.

PART II

*WHERE THE
SELVES MET*

CHAPTER TEN

Novelty to Norm

CATEGORIZING INTENT

Unlike many of the great inventions throughout the ages, the digital realm has been a grassroots phenomenon, a mix of innovation, creativity, personal expression, and big tech. It evolved on its own, out of supply and demand. There is no single creator.

An understanding how our online existence grew from novelty to a proxy of ourselves, we'll first take a look at why the concept of a user evolved around us.

Because digital identities unfolded over time, and didn't have a single origin, the process was evolutionary. Some of its origins were altruistic, some neutral, others abhorrent.

Access Through Infrastructure

Making technology or connectivity widely reachable by individuals, organizations, or the public at large was (and is) a cornerstone of the development of the digital realm. Connectivity, accessibility, free Chromebooks for grade school students, government portals, corporate IT systems, public WiFi, library digital lending (e.g. OverDrive), and even COVID all played a role.

Establishing Presence Through Consumerism and Choice

The creation of new online entities, technologies, platforms, or apps lay the groundwork for digital interaction without defining an ultimate social impact. The range is wide. The "who" in this scenario might be a budding influencer, a startup company, a journalist, a celebrity, or a politician or a niche hobby group. The "what" might be a home internet account, a company's website, social media, a dot-com concept, a vlog, an IMDB listing, or countless others.

Simply Existing, Digitally

At this point, experimenting evolved into acceptance. A user at this level chooses to complete everyday tasks online like banking, grabbing a rideshare, and ordering food.

This is the time that users became comfortable with digital presence that was no longer limited to phones or apps, or even things they voluntarily did. It was already embedded in industrial automation. AI and computer vision systems in warehouses, supermarkets, and logistics networks made decisions on our behalf every day. They adjusted supply chains, altered pricing, tracked the movement patterns of goods, and forecasted demand.

These systems recognized us, usually without us knowing it. They shaped what we see, what we pay, and what became available to us. No input required.

Induction into Selfhood

The encouragement of users to engage, contribute, personalize, or embed themselves within technological ecosystems, to become a contributor. Millions began with a social media account. Some blogged. We willingly created accounts that went beyond practical, no longer confining our online presence to activities like banking or work.

We leaned into personalization in this stage. We liked and followed. Depending on our demographic, we might have done TikTok challenges, Reddit AMAs, Words with Friends, FarmVille or Candy Crush.

Even charities and religious institutions created membership-based groups and presences to draw like-minded people in.

Altering Perception

The subtle reshaping of reality, identity, and trust through digital mediation, modified how individuals see themselves, others, or the world. It homogenized style and trends with its geographic reach. Some used beauty apps (e.g. Facetune), some became influencers and others followed them. Celebrities leveraged social media to manage their public persona, Instagram filters, Pinterest boards or Tumblr aesthetics, and countless corporate branding strategies are all examples of how the digital world took shape around us.

Reinforcing Dependence

Once we were there, the goal was to keep us there. This led to new innovations. Some were more benign, others deliberately addictive.

Examples include any innovation created exclusively to encourage habit-forming behavior. An entire category evolved that was specifically designed to create dependence. Algorithmic reinforcement (YouTube autoplay, infinite scroll), Snapchat streaks, YouTube "watch next" queue, and habit-forming interfaces (notifications, streaks, engagement loops) are all examples.

Ambient Legibility

The collection of data about our behavior through algorithms embedded in each one of the previous categories became an entrenched part of our online presence. The result was legibility. The legibility was of us. We opted in, sometimes justifying doing so by claiming we wanted safety, personalization, or convenience, whatever was being offered.

This form of observation becomes normalized over time. It could feel either benign or vaguely Orwellian, depending on context and control.

We felt comfortable with Alexa voice data, Google Maps location history, Ring doorbells, traffic cams, smart TVs that monitor usage, and mobile devices that track location in the background.

We were less comfortable with things like gated content, which is a link on the internet that forces you to enter your name, email and other information to create an account before you're allowed to read it. Still, we wanted to read it more than we really cared.

Exploiting Privacy

Here's where things got dark. We began to experience the crossing of ethical boundaries where personal data, identity, or presence is harvested, surveilled, or monetized without full consent or transparency.

Countless bad actors focused their attention online, realizing they could scam at unprecedented scale. They designed and built tools for an entirely new arena of crime. Examples include spying, hacking, data breaches, the Cambridge Analytica scandal, profile hijacking, impersonation, fake product reviews or followers, bots impersonating humans, and spearfishing (a targeted online scam where someone pretends to be a trusted person or organization to trick an individual into giving up sensitive information or clicking a harmful link. It's more personal than general phishing).

The Manipulation of Data

At the same time, a steady stream of news stories began to alert us to the commonplace, but deliberate, distortion or fabrication of truth within digital spaces through deceptive practices. Examples include viruses and malware, election interference, spyware, deepfakes, altered imagery in publications, the malicious use of AI to mislead or fabricate, knowingly fake news outlets, and more. When dishonest people discovered that they could profit from these, they developed tools and strategies that played an unfortunate role in the development of the digital world.

There will be some overlap with certain things falling into more than one category. The categories are non-linear; a lot of these conditions developed simultaneously around us.

Together, this list illustrates the ongoing evolution of the digital world's intent.

It expands constantly in a layered fashion, with everyday reach, from nearly endless origins. The common denominator, the intent behind all of it, was to reach individuals at scale.

CHAPTER ELEVEN

Search Results

INDICATORS OF PERSONHOOD

We live in an era in which unprecedented innovations are spreading through cultures, economies, and geographies over a relatively short period of time.

We'll always be physical beings, first. Society is rapidly moving online. A completely new phenomenon, sociologically speaking.

In the previous chapter, we studied why societal meanings, behaviors, and markers of identity have evolved in both the physical and digital realms, as a result of the digital age. In this chapter, we'll study how.

In many cases, attracting an audience requires providing some sort of incentive or reward for their participation. For that reason, the ways we were enticed to participate are positive, or are at least presented that way.

Access to Information and Education

UNESCO found in 2020 that online learning tools during the pandemic provided continued access for over 1.5 billion students globally.

In 2018, a study by the World Bank documented that literacy and numeracy improvements resulted when low-income children gain controlled digital access.

Commercially, companies like Apple donate millions of iPads to schools for several strategic reasons. None of them are purely philanthropic, although they are framed that way. Instead, their goal is early brand imprinting. When children grow up using Apple devices in school, they develop familiarity and emotional comfort with the interface. As a result, they're far more likely to remain Apple users for life. Donations are also tax write-offs. Educators look the other way and ignore the fact that Apple (and, to be fair, others) are preying on tiny children for their own gain, because the donation is too large and helpful for them refuse.

Health and Telemedicine

Remote diagnostics and telehealth have improved access in rural and underserved areas.

In 2021, the American Medical Association, found that 80% of physicians reported telehealth improved care.

Wearables and health apps have also increased preventive care and chronic illness monitoring, particularly in patients with diabetes. Fall detection and heart rate monitoring save lives.

These are mostly beneficial. But cookies and trackers are still embedded in telehealth sessions. Most hospitals are for-profit organizations. Wearables are marketed commercially for us to buy. As of 2024, the global wearable technology market, which includes smartwatches, fitness trackers, smart glasses, and other connected wearables, was valued between $70 billion and $178 billion.

Social Connectivity, Hobbies, Interests and Support

Digital platforms can reduce loneliness, especially among the elderly and disabled. The Pew Research Center reported in 2018 that social media use correlated with reported increases in perceived emotional support.

Marginalized communities often find identity validation, advocacy networks, or solidarity online.

The rest of us willingly participate for a wide variety of reasons.

For every user, the desire to participate comes from ourselves and our peers, as well as ads, clickbait and various other methods.

Deceptive Practices

Bad actors began to dangle virtual carrots for the purpose of drawing people in, so they could be taken advantage of. They targeted the lonely and vulnerable, the elderly and children. Their goal could be financial, sexual or violent.

They, too, use various means to entice us to engage.

Economic Mobility and Global Participation

Everything from stock trades, to your financial portfolio, to online banking is more convenient when done online.

Access to digital markets enables micro-entrepreneurship and gig work.

The World Bank Global Findex Database reported in 2021 that 1.2 billion people gained access to formal banking through mobile platforms over the last decade who previously had none.

This is a revolutionary shift, and while primarily positive, financial institutions do profit from interest they charge, and platforms benefit from a larger customer base.

Emergency Response

The smartphone radically altered the way we respond when in crisis. Originally, cellular phones had trouble with 911 calls because they lacked location precision, and no infrastructure was in place to provide the data to first responders. In 1996, the FCC adopted rules requiring wireless carriers to support E911 services. Mobile carriers had to provide the caller's phone number and the location of the cell tower that handled the call.

Under federal regulation, location sharing for 911 calls is mandatory and does not require user consent. It's one of the few exceptions to typical location privacy controls. We did not opt in, and we can't opt out. Even if we disable location services, emergency location access is still permitted by federal law.

It didn't take long before the technology was being used before you dialed 911. While the FCC's E911 regulations were not initially intended to enable police tracking of individuals, soon after, law enforcement started using location data to track individuals' locations as well.

Forced Participation

The requirement to use a certain app or online method forced many to migrate to digital platforms they didn't choose. For example, Turnitin (Turn it In) is a site where students submit papers. They are then checked for plagiarism by comparing submissions to a massive database of academic work, web pages, and student papers. Turnitin is considered the industry standard for academic integrity checks in schools and universities globally. Students are typically not given an alternate method to turn in their work, so their course grade is dependent on their use of Turnitin.

One of the major platforms for digital concert ticketing is the AXS App. To get your ticket, you have to download the app, install it, and create an account. On event day, you open the app and show your AXS Mobile ID, which is a rotating, scannable QR code that updates to prevent fraud. Often, you will have purchased your ticket from the concert website, not knowing that this process will be required for you to claim, or even sell, a ticket that probably cost you hundreds of dollars.

Many companies now use proprietary hiring platforms that require applicants to create an account, upload personal data, and agree to automated screening terms. You cannot submit a resume or apply without going through the portal. Most platforms even block uploads and require manual entry of all or part of your resume. Alternative application methods (email, in-person) are typically disallowed, especially at mid- to large-scale employers.

THOSE AT RISK

For some, added another layer to our already busy days. Others were a direct target. For others, it erodes identity from within. The psychological symptoms are recognizable: addictive behavior, alienation, depression. What begins as adaptation becomes destabilization.

While digital duality impacts nearly everyone, it does not affect everyone equally. The pressures of presence, and identity calibration vary sharply across lines of gender, race, and cultural background.

Experts still do not know how this condition will shape developing minds.

Teenage girls are often the first to show the psychological toll of online life. Not because they are weaker, but because the systems target them more aggressively and reward them less consistently. The social cost can be high, with little or no margin for error, and even their safety at stake.

Likewise, people of color and immigrants are asked, implicitly and explicitly, to "translate" themselves online: softening dialect, editing tone, proving relatability before authority is granted. A 2023 Pew Research Center study found that 56 percent of Black and Hispanic teens feel pressure to appear "cool" or "popular" on social media, compared to 39 percent of white teens.

These groups, more vulnerable or marginalized, become early warning systems for a deeper cost: a subtle erosion of internal coherence. We saw this long before the effects started to become universal.

It is not uncommon for people to behave differently behind a keyboard. There are internet trolls among us. We just have no idea who they are IRL (in real life).

What is at stake for everyone, even those with the lightest digital footprint, is not loss of attention or focus. It is the boundary between the internal and the external, between presence and performance, between time that is lived and time that is tethered elsewhere.

FROM SINGULAR TO SPLIT

Once it was enough to be. Now we must be twice, and still belong to ourselves, with one soul, and zero instructions. I don't know about you, but I hadn't even found myself yet. Now there are two. I'm still not even sure if this t-shirt goes with these jeans.

There was a point, somewhere between writing backend code and watching users interact with what I helped build, where it clicked: the systems had started shaping people, and most of us didn't even know it. They shaped users even when I hadn't included syntax in my own code to do so. It had more to do with where my code ended up (online, embedded in platforms that kept evolving), than my work alone.

I saw the gap widen between what someone was and how they were read. I knew the feeling because I had lived it. None of this came from theory. It came from my close-up and personal view of the systems we all use every day, and realizing they had more power than anyone expected, including me.

There were no experts. No maps. No TED Talks. Not even a Reddit thread to explain how to adapt to the relatively new worlds in which we exist.

Back in the day, which could mean ten minutes ago in this fast-paced world, but is probably more like 2007 (give or take), we used traditional markers to gauge identity, merit and value. You were all about your college degree, your job title, your IQ score. Status and prestige were institutionalized. The generations that came before us had inherited scaffolds of self-worth that didn't change much (or at all) for several centuries.

A quick comparison will illustrate just how significant of a shift that represents. Let's explore:

Your Home

Where you lived used to indicate stability, taste, financial standing. Now? You could be filming viral skincare routines from a mattress on the floor in a rented apartment and still wield more influence than someone with a five-bedroom house and a mortgage. Or, you could have leveraged that skincare routine into a house in Montecito near Oprah, but not have the education or work ethic to match.

The tricky part? You can't honestly say, "Home is no longer a status symbol or a marker of a certain identity." Home can still absolutely be a status symbol, until it's just a backdrop.

Your Job Title

Tack on "Director" or "VP" and it used to mean something. Those who held the title were. Those who didn't, aspired. It was about having realized something. Having actualized something.

Today, a person might have no official title at all and still reach an audience of millions. A successful creator, consultant, or freelancer may never use the word "director" or "vice president," yet operate with more influence and autonomy than those who do.

And sometimes, even those who carry the title don't hold the authority. In a recent federal case, a union petitioned to add fourteen Associate Vice Presidents to an existing group of union members. The law has always said that managers and supervisors can't be in unions. Surprisingly, the National Labor Relations Board ruled that these Associate Vice Presidents were not supervisors. Despite the title, they didn't meet the legal definition. They had enough in common with the rest of the unit to join.

Not long ago, most of us would have assumed that anyone with "Vice President" in their title automatically qualified as a supervisor. The gap between title and function is growing. The shape of success has changed. The language around it has not kept up.

Taking this a step further, if you don't broadcast your achievements, they don't count as much. Visibility has become part of validation. The quietest forms of success are often the least recognized.

You were promoted? They gave you a brand-new title? Don't forget to hop on LinkedIn and update your profile. You're an actor, or an author? Where's your website?

This shift echoes what Postman warned about in the television era: that public life was turning into performance. Social media has taken this further. Everything, even credibility, risks becoming a kind of entertainment.

Credibility hasn't disappeared. It's just dual now.

Your Wardrobe

Designer labels used to separate classes. Now? Minimalism is status. Vintage is bespoke. Fakes are everywhere. Thrift is aesthetic. As we entered the dot-com era, for the first time, finery didn't mean status or wealth. We watched as the unassuming man on the subway with a backpack ended up being richer than the man in Armani who just rolled up in a black sedan with a driver.

A 2020 Business of Fashion report noted that streetwear and normcore gained legitimacy not through runways, but via online communities, Instagram, and YouTube creators. Real people were dressing for the camera, not the corner office. Their relatability made viewers want to copy them. It had more appeal than a large fashion house did, telling us what we should buy and how much we should spend.

The shift was already in progress, then the pandemic accelerated it: performance above the waist. According to a 2021 McKinsey & Company report on post-pandemic fashion trends, companies like Stitch Fix and Nordstrom saw sharp increases in requests for "video call appropriate" tops and a plummet in formalwear sales.

On dating apps, professional platforms, and social media, first impressions now happen virtually. A 2023 Pew study on Gen Z identity found that 60% of respondents cared more about their profile photos than their physical presentation in everyday life.

In some cultures, labels still reign. In others, they've become gauche, cheap even. Quiet luxury and normcore have emerged. Again, the catch is that a designer wardrobe can still be a sign of status... or not.

Your Education

Degrees were currency, both figuratively and literally. Now, meritocracy has shifted in some fields, from credentials to skills and hustle. The smartest voice in the room might be self-taught. The person with the title might just be immensely charismatic, while being competent enough to bluff their way through. Meanwhile, Ivy League grads are quietly updating their resumes in co-working spaces. The confusing bit is that some expertise escaped the institution. Some didn't.

I knew a teenager, let's call him Travis. He was raised in Hinsdale, Illinois, a small neighborhood just outside of Chicago that I'd categorize as upper-class. Or at least the highest end of middle class. It was the kind of small town, locked in by other suburbs surrounding it, where everyone knows one another. I remember Travis well. He was a skinny kid, in a frayed baseball cap, with darker features and a thin-lipped, ready, wry smile.

Both of Travis' parents had very successful careers. They lived in one of the countless mini-mansions in town and drove luxury vehicles. In that local high school, the juniors and seniors talked about which colleges they were applying to. There was no "if". Just which ones.

Travis was somewhat of a self-taught tech prodigy. He'd spend afternoons in his room teaching himself code in several languages. Around 2010, maybe a little earlier, before TikTok but after Facebook stopped being cool, Travis got the email.

Nobody was surprised, but everyone was impressed. He had been accepted to the University of Illinois Urbana-Champaign (UIUC). Maybe you're aware of the school's Grainger College of Engineering and Department of Computer Science. They're consistently ranked among the top programs nationally and globally.

After about a year at UIUC, Travis was bored. He dropped out of college and entered the working world. The reaction of the small community was interesting. What would once have been the noise of endless gossip was just the silence of everyone holding their breath. Was this the story of a young person who just blew up his life? Up to now, that is what it surely would have meant. Had things really changed that much?

The answer, of course, is yes. Travis went on to pursue a rewarding and lucrative career. Travis didn't just step off the track. The track still exists. He simply proved there was another way forward. A new way. The community watched in quiet surprise as the world didn't collapse. Instead, it opened.

Your Car

Once the ultimate flex. Now it could mean debt. Meanwhile, the person next to you at the light in a 2008 Corolla has a crypto portfolio, a merch line, and 200,000 followers. The shift here has been notable. In the 80s, you looked like a god pulling up in a Lambo. I won't say what you look like now, let's just say it's "not the same". Status got unparked. The cool car always belongs to the antagonist in the movie now. The reasons may be numerous. Here's where duality comes in; if you're not physically pulling up to a building, nobody sees your car. What they do see is your $10,000 NFT avatar.

Your Friends

Friendship used to be measured in presence: who showed up, who called, who knew your coffee order. Now it's followers, likes, and DMs, even if you feel lonelier than ever. Or, you can be a loner "in real life" (IRL), but immensely popular behind a keyboard. We can't look at a person anymore and know.

Even something as simple Venmo is a statement. We proudly add something witty to the description, just to show the world where we were, when.

> Michael Constantine paid Amanda Trombetta (1d): 🍺 💃
>
> Joe Flatley paid Patrick Matthews (1d): squares
>
> Alex Leslie paid Britteny Knox (1d): 🍕
>
> Adriana Yu paid Sanctuary Holistic (2d): Yoga 🙏

It's both funny and a bit tragicomic that we turn even mundane financial transactions into mini social broadcasts.

I've never seen anyone put "mole removal", "roach extermination", or "toilet snake rental" here. For those, we slide the little bar from public to private before we press "pay."

Your Tech

When television was invented, it was a humble brag to admit you stayed up late watching. It meant you had access to something new. You were doing well. Today, if someone mentions they were up all night gaming or scrolling, it feels different. We worry about their productivity, their health. We might even interpret it as a lack of self-control.

The first widely available personal computer, the IBM PC, debuted in 1981 with a base model starting at $1,565. Adjusted for inflation, it would cost $5523.04 in 2025. A Compaq portable, a predecessor to the laptop computer, was $2995 in 1982. In 2025, that's roughly equivalent to $9956.28.

The Compaq Portable folded into a case about the size of a small carry-on suitcase. It weighed around 28 pounds, and had a 9-inch monochrome CRT screen. MS-DOS only, no Windows.

If you were seen walking into a high-rise office building or through an airport with one, it was assumed you were a serious business professional, probably an executive, consultant, or tech-savvy entrepreneur. It was a symbol of high status and forward-thinking. Very few people had personal computers at the time, let alone one they could carry. The sight of someone hauling a 28-pound "portable" PC into a meeting signaled that they were operating on the cutting edge of business technology.

Today, elementary students are given iPads or Chromebooks. Mid-level professionals, associates, analysts, sales reps, sometimes even interns, are handed a laptop when they start their job. Small children have smartphones.

It's common for gamers to invest in high-end systems used only for play, due to society's re-prioritization of the importance of tech.

Having certain cutting-edge tech devices might still mean you're doing well. On the other hand, since phones, laptops, and tablets have become manufacturing commodities, you can be walking around with the same devices used by presidents, celebrities and CEOs.

ADAPTATION

We are inhabiting two overlapping states, in real time, likely without conscious entry and exit from either, we're splitting our attention, and ourselves. And unlike a book or a television screen, the version of us that remains online continues to speak in our absence. It listens when we are silent, moves when we are still, and continues speaking long after we've stopped. It is constructed from choices we don't remember making, shaped by messages we didn't mean to send, and refined by systems we cannot see. Structurally, the two are different.

Fig. 11:1 Legacy Distractions vs. Digital Duality
Illustrating that we are not switching contexts; we are maintaining two at once.

OLD MEDIA (BOOKS, TV)	DIGITAL DUALITY
Require a clear decision to enter	Unprompted, ambient, and ongoing
Confined to specific contexts (you sit down to read or watch)	Unfolds across multiple contexts at once
The interruption is bounded: you know when you've exited	Infinite, not constrained by linear time
Passive	Responsive & declarative
Non-reciprocal	Bidirectional
Ends when you stop engaging	Continues even after you've looked away
Socially neutral	Socially consequential
Consumed as yourself	A second persona, different from the one you physically present

BIFURCATION

Historically, when society has evolved, we have moved on to whatever came next. We left behind the sensibilities of the Victorian era, the optimism of postwar modernism, the disillusionment of postmodern thought. Humans adapted through the eras, each generation different from the one before it, often without realizing we had done so.

Yet, the old ascribed social categories remained mostly intact as we moved from oral storytelling to print, from village economies to industrial cities, from landlines to mobile phones.

These social constructs haven't vanished. The key distinction is that their meaning is no longer a given in the same, concrete way it had been for centuries. A new duality has emerged for the first time. The challenge is, mindfulness-based approaches aim to restore attention to the present moment. But in the proxy condition, the moment itself is bifurcated. One cannot 'return to the present' when presence is simultaneously distributed. We must re-engineer what presence even means.

THE UNITY THRESHOLD

We haven't replaced the old identity structures; we've pushed them to one side, making room for a second set alongside the first. Since we weren't really aware that was taking place, we unknowingly risked the two parts becoming half of what they once were. A second persona, more fluid and elusive, now would move in parallel: curated, performed, and projected. It doesn't reside in brick or title. It is built from output, perception, and pace. Now, we don't merely have this second self. We're expected to maintain it in real time, all the time, without losing the first one.

Unlike the physical self, this one comes with no sociological precedence, no threshold, and no off switch.

Here are some ways in which these modern intangibles of performed selfhood are present in our daily lives:

Presence

This list is in no particular order, but I felt compelled to put this first, due to the sheer gravity of the concept.

You used to know if someone was with you or with someone else. Now, there are multiple layers to consider.

Someone can appear completely alone, yet be in the middle of a deeply felt exchange with an old friend. That friend might live nearby, or across the world. They might have met once, or never at all. They can laugh together, feel understood, even feel loved—without a single physical gesture. All while sitting alone in a room.

My teenage niece, and many of her friends, rarely leave their rooms outside of school hours. Yet in their minds, they have active social lives and are considered popular.

You might see a couple in a restaurant, both staring at their phones. You might assume distance. But what if they just finished a meaningful conversation and are now helping each other search for the same answer?

What if presence, once defined by proximity, has become a matter of intent? Presence is no longer absolute. It is relational and partitioned.

Sherry Turkle, an MIT sociologist who has written extensively on the impact of technology on human relationships, observed this shift more than a decade ago. We sit beside one another, but our minds, and often our meaning, are elsewhere.

As Turkle saw it, we may be physically co-present, but we withdraw into devices, trading rich, face-to-face interaction for shallow digital connection. Presence, for her, is defined as relational authenticity grounded in physical proximity and attentional focus. When someone is texting during dinner, or scrolling while listening, they are not "really there."

The idea that devices are harmful has been the position of scholars for years. Many still believe that. They definitely can be.

Of the hundreds of sources I've cited in this book, Turkle is on top of the list for groundbreaking insight. I consider it a springboard for this book. Without her, and others, you wouldn't be reading this now.

Knowledge is always a progression, especially when something is new and relatively unknown.

What we've come to realize since 2011-2015, when she laid the foundation for these concepts, is that all digital activity is not harmful. The state of being "not really there", is not inherently bad. Now that we better understand our digital presence, we've come to realize that logic is not universal. It's just not that black and white. There must be millions of reasons why someone can be with you, where you'd want them to be scrolling on their smartphone. Maybe you asked them for someone's number, or to send you an article the two of you were discussing.

One such example came up recently when I was having dinner with friends. The couple has two sons. One is in high school; we'll call him Liam. His older brother Logan had just started his freshman year at a university out of state.

At the restaurant, Liam was looking at his phone. His mother gave him the side eye, then glanced at his screen and shook her head. A silent shorthand for, "Get off the phone while we're at the table."

Liam looked up and smiled. "I got a YouTube alert. Logan's study group just won the hackathon."

His mom was smiling now. "Let's see," said his dad, extending a hand across the table to reach for Liam's phone.

Liam opened the video: a casual clip Logan had posted earlier that day and played it for his parents. In it, Logan stood in the campus library beside his team. They were holding up a cardboard sign that read Innovation Sprint Champions. Cheers, high-fives, laughter.

The video had just posted, but it didn't appear at random. Liam had watched Logan's other updates, liked one, commented on another. That pattern of attention had trained the system to recognize Logan as meaningful to Liam specifically.

So when Logan's video went live, the platform surfaced it instantly. Logan didn't send it and Liam didn't search for it. Their connection had become structurally legible. It was now part of the system's logic.

At that moment, Logan was present, acted through. The system treated him as a referent identity. It didn't need his input to reintroduce him. And it didn't need Liam to go looking.

That is the proxy condition: presence without prompting.

Still, the truth is, we never could judge presence by physicality alone. Even before everyone walked around with a smartphone in their hand, someone could be sitting next to you smiling, and nodding, and be miles away in their mind. Attention can be illusory.

What's changed is how that presence is recorded, then acted upon. Using philosophical anchoring, one could argue that a cassette tape recording of your voice could be triggered without your attention, parsed without your consent, acted through without your awareness, and referenced in future decisions made by non-human agents.

A cassette tape is static. It doesn't change based on how it was used last time. It is played. It doesn't play back differently depending on who listens or when. A cassette can be changed, but it cannot change itself.

A tape only contains your voice. A proxy acts as your voice.

CULTURAL SOCIOLOGY OF PRESENCE

Next, let's study how societal meanings, behaviors, and markers of identity have evolved in both the digital and physical realms, as a result of the digital age:

Confidence

It used to show in how someone walked into a room. Now confidence can be faked, captioned, filtered, and scheduled for peak visibility. You can radiate insecurity and still look bulletproof online. To some degree, self-assurance is now aesthetic. Yet, the legacy metrics of identity are still very much alive. The same person. Two worlds.

Belonging

You once belonged to a place, a group, a neighborhood. Now you "join" a thousand things but really belong to none. Or, you can be well adjusted and connected in life, but feel like an absolute alien at family Thanksgiving dinner.

Success

Success used to be finishing something. Building something. It still can be. But it can also be perception. A photo shoot can look like a business. A soft launch can outrun reality. Meanwhile, quiet success goes unnoticed because it isn't optimized for virality.

We've talked about the kind of people who were once considered successful. They were institutional achievers. They were the benchmark. With few exceptions, it mattered little what kind of human they were. They had arrived. That was enough. But achievement is no longer a finish line. Even if you get there, reverence is not guaranteed.

Every tweet (or whatever it's called now), every viewpoint, every offhand comment is tallied. Success has become inseparable from surveillance.

You can build an empire now, and still be, let's face it, a bit of a joke.

Sincerity

Your voice really was your password. It could evoke sincerity, danger, warmth, seriousness, sarcasm, humor, awkwardness, hope, fear, and joy. Now, sincerity can be scripted. A moment that once meant everything in person can now feel like content. Rehearsed. Edited. Maybe even monetized.

Some things we once relied on as indicators of truth are no longer there. Texts between friends can easily be misinterpreted without tone to carry meaning. An email sent to half a dozen co-workers can be taken six different ways.

Rest

Perhaps the most visceral change of all. We used to rest. Now we log off. But our digital self stays awake; liking, tagging, getting analyzed, sold, scraped. There is no stillness anymore, only disconnection disguised as peace.

We stay up later than we should, with digital activity being the sole cause. We wake in the middle of the night and reach for our phones. We do this knowing that the loss of restful sleep quickly impacts mental health and well-being. We'll be exhausted at work or school tomorrow. We keep scrolling, gaming, chatting anyway.

We have become a restless society, as sleep scientists and psychologists have increasingly observed, one that can no longer truly relax. This is more than burnout. It is a cultural phenomenon. A cost to the collective psyche.

FoMO, the fear of missing out, has made rest feel less like idleness and more like absence. Worse, the digital dopamine loop often makes the virtual feel more rewarding than what we once called real.

As Dr. Anna Lembke writes, "Dopamine is not about pleasure, but about the anticipation of reward. That anticipation keeps us scrolling, swiping, and clicking. Not because it feels good, but because it might."

SOCIETY HAS A NEW GENRE

The proxy line is a cognitive and cultural state in which digital experiences occur alongside direct experience, impacting both how people relate to themselves and to others. It's an additional, second state of being. One that has developed in us, as a society, over the past twenty or so years.

Now, web-based systems coincide with our physical consciousness, which has always been there. In this new social reality, metrics, notifications, and public feedback have begun to shape our sense of identity alongside physical experience.

Digital life, at this point, is so ingrained in us that to deny yourself this condition would mean to sit on the sidelines of humanity. This dual existence enhances us, if it is managed with intention.

The proxy condition is not only the result of technological change but also reflects a broader shift in how knowledge, identity, and value are constructed. It redefines what we see as "real" and begins to separate performance from participation in ways that are not easily discerned and impossible to reverse.

CHAPTER TWELVE
The Progression

ASSEMBLY REQUIRED

The logical-minded might (correctly) argue that we've always had distractions. That our attention has never belonged to us entirely. That even before the screen, we wandered. Books, radio, television. These, too, could pull us out of the moment, immerse us, take us away.

That argument is not wrong. But it is not complete.

What has changed is not our capacity to be drawn in. It is the nature of absorption itself.

We are no longer simply pulled into a story or a song. What has shifted is not just the volume of noise, but the nature of involvement. Our personality now develops along two axes: the physical and the digital. Each requires its own instincts. This new state demands a new kind of coherence that was never needed before.

BEYOND ADOPTION AT SCALE

When new tools are introduced, we call it a milestone. When it changes what a self is, we call it evolution.

What these eras show us is that we've experiences much more than just mass digital use. The adoption of technology brought with it embedded legibility, recurrence, and autonomy within ambient systems. It is a roadmap to the proxy condition. If we can't opt out, what does a dual existence look like?

It appears that the only way forward is to look carefully at this new reality, and decide how we'd like to shape it, and how we'd like it to shape us.

Since we can't reject the proxy self, we'll accept and manage it instead.

If we are inhabiting two overlapping states, in real time, without conscious exit from either, we're splitting our attention, and ourselves. And unlike a book or a television screen, the version of us that remains online continues to speak in our absence. It listens when we are silent, moves when we are still, and continues speaking long after we've stopped.

It is constructed from choices we don't remember making, shaped by messages we didn't mean to send, and refined by systems we cannot see. Over time, it may become clearer to others than the version we physically present of ourselves. It is structurally different, but alive.

THE DIGITAL TRANSFORMATION

Twenty or so years ago, technology was typically embraced by a higher-educated, predominantly white male crowd.

Now, we can text, control our thermostat, order Starbucks, pay for lunch, watch a video, check our bank balance, and get Walmart delivered to our doorstep, all in under an hour.

In developed nations, all demographics, from infancy to centenarians in nursing homes participates. All races, the majority of religions, at mostly every income level, all occupations, in rural areas, suburbs and cities alike. The majority of us actively participate. An overwhelming portion of the minority not included in these groups, also participate, albeit passively. We'll talk more about that in later chapters.

Settling into the digital realm, society drifts more toward a collective. Technology homogenizes trends, style, news cycles and cultural references. Influencers make it desirable to copy and emulate. A 2022 Pew study found Gen Z is less likely to list "individuality" as a top personal value than Millennials did at the same age:

Then: *"Be yourself. Be original. Stand out."*

Now: *"Be aspirational. Be relatable. Be followed."*

TikTok and Instagram trends show mass synchronous behavior (e.g., lip-syncing, dances, quote-sharing), favoring precision imitation over personalization. YouTube experimented with thumbnail images to see which ones people clicked on most. Over time, this trained creators to follow the same winning formula. Bright faces, bold text, exaggerated expressions. The more it worked, the more it spread. Gradually, everything started to look the same. Creativity is reverse-engineered through what works, not what inspires.

We are even integrating devices into our physical bodies. Wearables read our pulse and track our heart rate. Smart glasses record what we see. Some seem like voices in our head. There is much to gain, but we do we lose pieces of our individuality. A modern-day version of Star Trek's Borg?

Can wearing an Apple Watch or watching a few reels really erode individuality? Probably not today. But as the YouTube thumbnails example shows, over time, constantly syncing ourselves to external systems will begin to socially flatten the range of our idealized behavior and priorities.

You may have already noticed certain cultural trends shaped by devices and their feedback loops. They do have the ability to nudge us into acting alike.

One of the most recognizable examples is the Fitbit step goal. The idea that 10,000 steps a day ensures health and fitness is a myth. It began in 1965 as a marketing campaign for a Japanese pedometer called the Manpo-kei. The name translates roughly to "10,000 steps," chosen not for scientific reasons, but because it was simple, memorable, and easy to sell. Yet, how many people view it as an ideal daily goal?

There is even tribalism around which tools we use. iPhone versus Android. Strong opinions have formed about each.

A grandmother standing in line at the supermarket, and a young man behind her might both use the same brand phone and feel connected, despite being two distinctly different people. Two close friends sitting together on a bench at school might find themselves divided by which phone they hold.

As I began to consider the impact of events like these, it became clear that we've been living through a redefinition of what it means to be human in a networked world.

The proxy condition did not emerge suddenly. It was cultivated, layer by layer. Technological events rewired our expectations, blurred our sense of coherence, and quietly changed the rules of daily life.

To study these layers, I found it helpful to map out some of the most pivotal milestones of the past twenty years.

What follows is a record of how the digital age has reshaped the conditions for trust, identity, and participation itself. I've separated them into individual eras. These will vary slightly, depending upon who you ask, but the digital age runs roughly along these lines:

1987 to 1995: Inception

We cross over the digital threshold. Early systems emerge, and the groundwork is laid for a new mode of interaction.

1995 to 2006: Emergence

We witness the rise of the online self. Identity begins to migrate online, shaped by social platforms, commerce, and personalization.

2007 to 2015: Integration

Many everyday tasks migrate over to the internet. Mobile, social, and platform ecosystems absorb everyday activity. Digital life becomes preferred.

2016 to 2020: Consciousness

Growing awareness of surveillance, manipulation, and data vulnerability challenges early optimism.

2021 to Present: Automation

AI-generated content and synthetic experiences become part of our lives.

The internet ranks at or near the top of any list you'll find of the most transformative inventions in human history.

When humans learned out to create a fire, it extended waking hours, and saved lives by providing heat and cooking food that would have been dangerous to eat raw.

Timekeeping, through mechanical clocks and calendars enabled science, commerce, labor, and ushered in a new era of reliability.

Agriculture made settlements, cities, and accessibility to resources possible.

Writing enabled memory, law, history, and organized religion. Later, the printing press spread that information to masses, which spread knowledge and enlightenment.

The wheel made all mechanical movement possible.

Airplanes completely redefined geography, making it feasible for humans to travel to distant parts of the globe.

Invention of the telephone marked the age of instantaneous personal communication.

Penicillin shifted mortality and survival rates and ushered in modern medicine. Electricity elevated civilization to a new level, powering industry, cities, and communication.

As impactful as those events were, there are many who have argued that the digital age is number one on this list. Their reasoning? It converges and magnifies nearly all prior inventions. It has a systemic influence on nearly every domain of life: communication, commerce, education, politics, science, culture, and identity.

Another unique attribute is that internet is recursive. It is the only thing on this list that contributes to its own architecture and advancement. It is a tool that can build tools. It utilizes many of the world's previous inventions, like writing and timekeeping. It then contributes to nearly all the others, helping to facilitate heating and cooking (as fire did), keeping digital time, writing, printing, manufacturing wheels and airplanes, making voice communication possible through VOIP and other methods, making modern medicine safer and more reliable, and regulating electricity and other natural resources.

AI added yet another recursive layer. The internet enables AI, and AI rewrites how we use and evolve the internet.

Humans shape the internet with their thoughts, then reshape their thoughts through internet use. It is a loop not found in other inventions.

The internet also has no central origin or single inventor; mirroring how modern identity and authority have also decentralized. In doing so, it inverted power structures, empowering individuals in unprecedented ways.

The effects amplify over time, too. Every new user, service, or data stream expands what's possible, not just quantitatively but structurally.

In short, the others are tools, while the digital age is more of a metatool, capable of both enabling and accelerating paradigm shifts across all other domains.

I've built a timeline to illustrate that once-in-humanity shift. We are alive at a singular moment in human history that altered how we know, relate, and exist within the world. What follows is not just technological evolution; it is sociological transformation.

The scale of transformation we've lived through is hard to grasp. With that in mind, what follows is a hand-picked list of impactful events mapping technology's reshaping of human trust and identity, grouped by era.

Fig. 12:1 The Architecture of Digital Transformation: 1987 to 1995: Inception

tl/dr: Core technologies such as digital cameras, antivirus software, early internet protocols, and the World Wide Web began to emerge. Basic digital trust systems like HTTPS and online reviews took root. Personal use of the internet began, but remained limited.

YEAR*	MILESTONE	NOTES
1971	Email	Ray Tomlinson sends the first networked message between computers over ARPANET and introduces the "@" symbol for addresses.
1988	Digital Cameras	Fuji and Nikon launch digital cameras, setting the stage for free trial and error photography, after a century of printed photos.
1988	Antivirus Software	McAfee, Norton profit from defense against digital threats.
1988	Adobe Photoshop	Adobe Photoshop debuts, bringing powerful image-editing tools to personal computers and blurring the line between authentic and altered imagery.
1989	World Wide Web	Tim Berners-Lee proposes the World Wide Web (www), creating a hyperlinked information system. The Mosaic browser, Netscape Navigator and first websites follow, opening the internet to the public and making global digital presence possible, through a dial-up connection. Companies buy domain names.

YEAR*	MILESTONE	NOTES
1993	Oprah TV Guide Cover	Oprah's head is composited onto Ann-Margret's body without consent. An early media ethics breach and high-profile example of digital photo manipulation. It is followed by several more, including Britney Spears' retouched Elle cover (2004), and Andy Roddick's digitally enlarged physique on Men's Fitness (2007). Photo manipulation scandals expose how image editing quietly reshaped public trust in visual media. Altered images now define beauty norms, gender expectations, and media credibility.
1993	Firewalls	First developed in the late 1980s, firewalls become standard across businesses and institutions by the early 2000s, out of necessity. Cybersecurity forces their adoption into a baseline expectation and reframes the internet as a space that must be actively defended.
1994	WebCrawler	WebCrawler is introduced as the first full-text search engine.
1994	Amazon	Amazon launches, marking the beginning of the e-commerce boom.
1994	Yahoo	Yahoo introduces search, transforming how people search online and giving visibility to sites previously hidden to users.
1994	HTTPS	Netscape introduces secure online transactions, alerting the public for the first time that browsing had been largely insecure until then.
1995	eBay	eBay (originally AuctionWeb) launches, pioneering online marketplaces with user ratings (reviews/feedback). Anyone can list an item for sale. It normalizes commerce between strangers and builds trust in digital transactions. It completely transforms hobbies by establishing a transparent, data-driven marketplace that fosters price discovery and standardizes valuations, and connects larger communities of collectors. It helps fuel the growing interest in vintage home decor by making secondhand and collectible items more accessible to a broader audience.

YEAR*	MILESTONE	NOTES
1995	Match.com	Match.com, the first major dating website, goes live. A large portion of the dating public embraces it, marking a major shift to dating online, expanding the dating pool, and requiring people to craft profiles and trust virtual first impressions. Relationships and marriages result.
1995	Geocities is created	Birth of personal web pages and mass self-publication. Early proto-social media.
1995	First widespread malware ("Concept" Word macro virus)	Early proof that digital environments could be weaponized.

Do you remember, or have you heard, the sound of a dial-up modem? That screech and hum meant you were entering a world that didn't exist seconds earlier. You felt like you were disappearing from one reality and entering another.

Perhaps the most significant shift in this early era was the electronic message: email.

For centuries, long-distance communication had remained fundamentally unchanged, relying on letters carried by courier systems that evolved slowly from ancient Persia, Rome, and China. Email abruptly rewrote (pun intended) those expectations. It introduced immediacy, informality, and digital permanence into correspondence. It was, and is, the first instance of the always-on, digital-first environment we live in today.

Corporations were buying domain names, but there were still relatively few websites. Most computers weren't networked yet. They existed in isolation, and transferring large files or large amounts of data remained a challenge. Amazon was still just a small-ish online bookstore.

Yet, looking back, several other innovations were already reshaping how people interacted. eBay brought regular people into online commerce and began shaping hobbies and valuation norms in previously unheard-of ways. It even influenced home decor. Accessibility to re-sold items helped shape the vintage-forward interior design trends of the decades that followed. Ebay became, in a sense, an early influencer. Match.com, the first major dating site, fundamentally altered courtship for the first time in history. WebCrawler, the first full-text search engine, introduced true discoverability and changed how people navigated the internet. Prior to that, you had to know where you wanted to go, and type in the URL. Searchability meant that you could find information, instead of just looking up a site. It opened up the web.

In 1993, there were approximately 130 websites. By the end of 1995, there were approximately 23,500 websites on the internet. Many users were still browsers, and may or may not have possessed a single set of login credentials yet.

Viruses and digital threats began to surface, revealing early vulnerabilities in the system. Photo manipulation emerged as an ethical fault line in media. And the introduction of the first search engine, crude by today's standards, was nonetheless revolutionary.

At this point in time, we didn't possess a proxy condition. Digital tools were emerging, but they hadn't reshaped the self.

**Fig. 12:2 The Architecture of Digital Transformation
1995 to 2006: Emergence**

tl/dr: Search engine wars, e-commerce, and early social media platforms like Myspace, and LinkedIn tied online presence increasingly to real-world identity. Blogging culture and mobile phones emerge. Surveillance systems expand after 9/11. Personal identity takes shape in digital form.

YEAR*	MILESTONE	NOTES
1996	Mapquest	Customized route mapping becomes accessible online for the first time, although not yet dynamic or real-time.
1997	AOL Instant Messenger (AIM)	AIM launches, popularizing instant messaging with buddy lists and away messages, bringing casual, always-on communication into daily life.
1997	Netflix	Digital migration of entertainment; DVDs, then streaming.
1997	Online Banking	Wells Fargo launches the first online banking platform available to consumers; banking is available online.
1998	Google Search Engine	Google is founded, quickly becoming the go-to search engine for the web. The search wars begin.
1998	PayPal	Online payment systems normalize fast digital financial transactions and allow anyone to collect money online, without a credit card or a bank.
1998	GPS	Standalone GPS devices like Garmin and Magellan units enter the consumer market, and in-vehicle GPS emerges, offering real-time navigation in vehicles. Later (2009), mapping largely goes mobile (Google Maps and Waze).
1999	Blogging	Platforms like LiveJournal and Blogger launch, making it easy for anyone to start a blog. Millions begin publishing their thoughts and daily lives online, turning private diaries into public narratives. This marks the start of blogging culture and the idea of an online personal brand, as individuals curate identities and build audiences on the open web.

YEAR*	MILESTONE	NOTES
1999	Napster	Napster debuts, allowing users to share music files directly with each other. Its explosive popularity disrupts the music industry and shows the power of online communities to upend traditional business models. It also raises ethical and legal dilemmas about digital content ownership and the willingness of people to obtain media through unofficial networks. Major artists like Metallica, Dr. Dre sue. Later, in 2003, The Recording Industry Association of America (RIAA) is formed, and is criticized for aggressively suing individuals, including teenagers, college students, and even parents.
1999	Court E-Filing	Courts across the U.S. begin adopting electronic filing systems, allowing lawsuits, motions, and legal documents to be submitted online. Judicial trust, once embodied in physical paperwork and in-person verification, migrates into digital portals.
1999	Spyware	Malware like "Elf Bowling" enters mainstream culture, showing that even entertainment downloads can hide malicious software.
1999	Always-On Internet	DSL and cable replace dial-up. Customers are put on waiting lists as demand for always-on internet exceeds infrastructure capacity.
2000	Bill Paying	Banks and service providers offer online bill pay, drastically cutting paper mail volume. Administrative tasks shift to auto-pay systems, changing financial habits and fostering passive financial presence.
2000	eSignatures	The U.S. ESIGN Act legally recognizes electronic signatures, allowing contracts to be signed digitally. Trust, once tied to handwritten signatures and physical presence, shifts into the online space, making business, banking, and government transactions fully digital.

YEAR*	MILESTONE	NOTES
2000	Microsoft Antitrust	The U.S. Government investigates Microsoft for the bundling of Internet Explorer with the Windows operating system. Early government recognition of tech monopolies. The federal courts struggle to knowledgeably try the case, and to understand implications.
2000	First Ransomware	Malicious encryption (AIDS Trojan) begins to surface. Cyberattacks demonstrate the capability to shut down major corporations and institutions.
2000	DMV Services	State DMVs introduce online portals for vehicle registration renewal, address changes, and license services. A new expectation forms: that even core government functions involving identity verification and legal status should be self-managed digitally. It blurs the boundary between state authority and personal digital autonomy.
2000	PlayStation 2	Sony releases the PlayStation 2 (PS2), which becomes the best-selling gaming console of all time. Its success shifts video gaming from a niche hobby to a mainstream entertainment industry on par with film and music, deeply embedding interactive entertainment into digital culture and personal identity.
2000	Dot-com Bubble Burst	A stock market crash follows rapid investment in internet-related companies, peaking in March 2000. Irrational exuberance drives the NASDAQ Composite index to rise fivefold before a dramatic fall. The bust collapses many dot-com companies and erases significant market capitalization, exposing technology's role as a core driver of the global economy.
2001	Wikipedia	Wikipedia, a free crowd-sourced encyclopedia, goes online. It revolutionizes knowledge by allowing anyone to contribute or edit articles. The project's success demonstrates the viability of user-generated content and collective intelligence, while also prompting debates about accuracy since the authority of information is no longer centralized.

YEAR*	MILESTONE	NOTES
2001	Post-9/11 Surveillance	After 9/11, the USA PATRIOT Act dramatically expands government surveillance of digital communications. Internet and phone data become subject to increased monitoring. This trade-off between security and privacy brings to light how our digital lives can be observed and logged, fueling future concerns over who is watching and storing personal data.
2001	Google News	News consumption starts to move online. Algorithmic aggregation begins. Personalized feeds are criticized for their bias.
2001	Apple Retail Store	Apple opens its first retail stores, blending lifestyle branding with tech sales. It sets the template for future experiential retail.
2001	Anonymity Reshapes Online Behavior	Dark Web development (Tor Project) creates a hidden online environment used for illegal and nefarious purposes. The image board 4chan is created, allowing users to post completely anonymously. It becomes a breeding ground for both internet culture (memes like Rickrolling, LOLcats) and darker, trollish behavior.
2002	Online Voter Registration	States begin offering online voter registration. It improves access but introduces cybersecurity risks into election systems.
2002	Retail Loyalty Programs	Major retailers move loyalty programs online, normalizing the trade of personal information for discounts. Data becomes a new form of currency.
2003	Medical Records	Patient portals like MyChart debut, giving individuals remote access to health records, test results, and communication with doctors. Sensitive private information now lives online, transforming trust in medical privacy and redefining the management of personal health.

YEAR*	MILESTONE	NOTES
2003	Package Tracking	UPS, FedEx, and USPS launch real-time online package tracking for consumers. The ability to monitor deliveries minute-by-minute begins to recalibrate expectations of immediacy, transparency, and digital visibility, into broader life expectations for instant updates and surveillance.
2003	MySpace	MySpace launches and soon becomes the largest social networking site of its era. It lets users customize profiles with music, photos, and a personal page, and encourages them to collect large "friends" lists. MySpace brings social networking into the mainstream, especially for teenagers and musicians, making the personal profile a key mode of self-expression and status in the digital world.
2003	Skype	First widespread normalization of free global voice/video calls, reshaping personal communication. What was once imagined in SciFi had arrived.
2003	Linkedin	Professional identity construction moves online.
2004	World Of Warcraft	World of Warcraft (WoW), a massively popular multiplayer online role-playing game, launches and becomes a cultural phenomenon. Millions create characters in this fantasy world, forming guilds and spending countless hours on collective quests. WoW's success highlights how digital worlds can become deeply meaningful extensions of players' lives and identities. Some invest as much pride in their online accomplishments as in real-life ones.
2004	"Web 2.0" And User Content	"Web 2.0" gains prominence, describing the new wave of websites focused on participation and sharing (blogs, wikis, social media). Marks recognition that the web is no longer read-only: users are now active contributors, and the internet is a collaborative space where users define the experience.

YEAR*	MILESTONE	NOTES
2005	YouTube And Viral Video	YouTube is launched as a site for anyone to upload and share videos easily. It popularizes the idea of "viral videos" and empowers ordinary people to become content creators. With it, performing for a global audience becomes possible from one's bedroom, launching the era of YouTube celebrities and proving that user-generated video could rival traditional media in influence and reach.
2005	Google Acquires Android	Sets the stage for mass mobile computing and fragmented app ecosystems.
2005	Reddit	Reddit, a user-driven news aggregator and discussion platform, launches. It quickly becomes a hub for niche communities ("subreddits") and a powerful force in shaping internet culture, memes, and citizen journalism. By the 2010s, major news outlets cite Reddit threads as credible sources. Reddit's upvote system also influences later content ranking algorithms on social media.
2006	Google Buys YouTube	Consolidates power over video content, supercharging the rise of influencers and algorithm-driven visibility.
2006	Lonelygirl15 Hoax	A hugely popular YouTube vlogger known as "Lonelygirl15" is revealed to be an actress playing a role, not an actual teen sharing her life. The discovery that an apparently genuine online persona was fictional shocks fans. It's a wake-up call that not everyone (or everything) online is as it seems, sowing early seeds of skepticism about the authenticity of user-generated content and digital identities.
2006	Twitter And Hashtags	Twitter launches, introducing microblogging with 140-character posts. Its real-time feed and the invention of the hashtag create a new form of mass communication – concise, immediate public messaging. Twitter becomes a platform for personal expression, citizen journalism, and global conversations, where regular individuals can gain as much influence as traditional news outlets (but also where information can spread chaotically and without verification).

You sent your first instant message. Someone was on the other side, *typing back*. That blinking cursor was a heartbeat. We were learning to be present through text.

This was a pivotal era. When you look at all the innovation, that in itself says a lot. Rather than being slow to emerge, people were embracing the digital realm quickly.

By the end of this period, online life had begun to feel real, and personal. Not in a metaphorical sense, but in a way that quietly redefined what it meant to be known. Identity moved online. Not as a copy, but as a counterpart.

At this point, the majority of people with internet access had begun living in a digital world. By now, most of us had purchased a cell phone and a home PC, made an automated payment, purchased something online, read articles or books, tracked a package, sent a text, eSigned a document, or conducted other personal business over the internet.

Many of us were on social media.

Gaming was elevated to a new level with World of Warcraft.

Communication became casual. Community became clickable. In trading any mistrust we once had for ease and convenience, we allowed digital systems to take root not just in our habits, but in our sense of self, our identity.

In its most literal and functional sense, a timeline following the appointment of a proxy begins with a moment of disconnection or inability, which necessitates representation. That proxy then acts on behalf of the original source during a period of absence, silence, or incapacitation. For example, your brother is in the hospital, with both arms and both legs broken, following a skydiving mishap. He asks you to be his proxy voter.

By design, our physical selves are not able to represent us in the digital realm. At this point, we see the proxy condition begin to emerge. You are serving as a proxy for your physical self.

Fig. 12:3 The Architecture of Digital Transformation
2007 to 2015: Integration

tl;dr: The iPhone's release sparked the mobile-first era. Facebook, YouTube, Twitter, and later Instagram dominated. Personal branding, influencers, podcasting, and algorithmic visibility became monetized. Big Tech firms consolidated power across communications, commerce, and culture. We fully stepped into the digital world.

YEAR*	MILESTONE	NOTES
2007	Apple Iphone	The first iPhone redefines the mobile phone as a powerful handheld computer with internet, apps, and a touch interface. By putting the web, email, and a camera literally in people's hands at all times, the iPhone accelerates the blurring of online and offline life. Now the digital world travels with you, enabling constant sharing of photos, status updates, and real-time communication wherever you are. Mobile-first internet use begins.
2007	Kindle E-Reader	Digitizes books and personal libraries, changing how people read for the first time since the invention of Gutenberg's printing press, circa 1450.

YEAR*	MILESTONE	NOTES
2007	Facebook Platform & Apps	Facebook opens its platform to outside developers, allowing third-party apps and games to integrate (e.g. FarmVille, quizzes), to enormously popular response. This makes Facebook more than a social hub. It becomes a whole digital ecosystem, increasing engagement and new behaviors (like casual social gaming), but also quietly expands how much personal data flows to Facebook and app makers, foreshadowing later privacy issues from data-hungry apps.
2007	Influencers	Introduction of the YouTube Partner Program normalizes online content monetization, turning users into micro-brands. Influencers are born.
2008	Social Media In Obama Election	Barack Obama's presidential campaign leverages social media and data analytics at an unprecedented scale for organizing, fundraising, and voter outreach. This is the first major election where a candidate's digital strategy leverages the political power of social platforms and foreshadows their central role in future civic movements and elections.
2008	Chrome Browser	Google's grip on the web expands with the launch of the Chrome browser.
2009	WhatsApp	Privacy-centered messaging like WhatsApp gains popularity worldwide; shifts expectation for encrypted casual communication.
2009	Cars Become Connected	Car manufacturers begin integrating internet connectivity into vehicles, starting with services like GPS navigation updates, emergency response (e.g., OnStar), and remote diagnostics. Mobility itself becomes part of the digital web, introducing expectations of constant tracking, real-time service, and software-mediated driving experiences.

YEAR*	MILESTONE	NOTES
2009	Bitcoin And Blockchain	The first Bitcoin block is mined, kicking off the cryptocurrency revolution. Bitcoin introduces the idea of a decentralized digital currency that doesn't require any government or bank, relying instead on cryptography and a public ledger (blockchain) to establish trust. In addition to challenging traditional finance, Bitcoin sparks discussion about digital anonymity (users identified only by cryptographic addresses) and new forms of economic identity untethered from nations or banks.
2009	Facebook "Like" Button	Facebook deploys the "Like" button across its platform. This simple feature to express approval becomes a fundamental mode of online interaction, quantifying social feedback. It changes how people behave online – users begin chasing likes as a measure of validation, and algorithms use likes to tailor what content you see – deeply influencing self-esteem, content creation, and the reward system of social media.
2009	Uber and the Gig Economy	Uber begins operations, allowing users to order car rides via a smartphone app. It quickly popularizes the concept of on-demand services, matching strangers for transactions in real time. By relying on GPS tracking and two-way ratings for accountability, Uber changes trust models. Users become comfortable getting into a stranger's car because a digital platform vouches for it. It also sparks the broader gig economy, where one's livelihood can be managed through digital apps that link supply and demand for real-world services.
2009	Texting Overtakes Email	Except in business settings, where email is still the norm, text becomes the preferred method of communication.
2009	Twitter As News	All major news outlets start following and citing tweets as formal sources. Political communication (e.g., from U.S. congresspeople, global leaders) shifts visibly onto social media.

YEAR*	MILESTONE	NOTES
2009	Customer Service Moves To AI-Human Hybrids	Companies adopt live chat systems that begin blending human support with AI-driven bots. The expectation of service shifts: immediacy becomes prized over personal interaction. Digital assistance, once human-mediated, increasingly feels algorithmic, standardizing help into scripted, efficiency-first exchanges.
2010	Instagram	Instagram launches as a mobile photo-sharing app with built-in filters to beautify images. It rapidly gains popularity, fostering a culture of carefully curated, visually appealing life updates. Instagram accelerates the rise of the "influencer" and a culture where people craft idealized digital personas complete with followers and likes as metrics of success, shifting social media toward visual storytelling and personal branding.
2010	Wikileaks "Cablegate"	WikiLeaks publishes a massive trove of confidential U.S. diplomatic cables (after earlier leaks of war logs). The "Cablegate" leak exposes government secrets on a global scale, only possible via digital means. It's a milestone in transparency and whistleblowing powered by the internet, demonstrating how a small group can use digital platforms to hold powerful institutions accountable. It also raises complex questions about the line between public interest and national security in the digital age.
2010	GoFundMe	GoFundMe launches, normalizing personal crowdfunding for emergencies, medical expenses, education, and life events. Public appeals for financial help become part of one's online identity, as individuals curate narratives around need and worthiness for viral sharing. Digital trust metrics (shares, likes, donation counts) begin replacing traditional notions of community aid.

YEAR*	MILESTONE	NOTES
2010	Internet Of Things (IoT)	Home devices like Nest thermostats, Ring doorbells, and smart plugs enter mainstream adoption. Everyday objects, from security systems to light bulbs, washers, dryers and dishwashers, are connected, embedding constant surveillance, data collection, and remote control into private aspects of daily life.
2012	Voice-to-Text Finally Works	After decades of unreliable speech recognition, Google's neural network-based voice input delivers usable results. This milestone makes dictation, voice assistants, and live captioning viable, altering how people write, search, and interact with devices.
2011	Snapchat And Disappearing Content	Snapchat is released, pioneering ephemeral messaging – photos and videos that vanish after viewing. This design taps into a desire for more genuine, spontaneous sharing without the permanent record of traditional social media. It shifts how younger generations communicate, encouraging a more candid digital persona (silly snaps, in-the-moment shots) and influencing other platforms to later adopt "Stories" and disappearing posts as a way to keep interactions feeling lighter and more lifelike.
2012	Tinder And Swipe Culture	Tinder launches, introducing the swipe-right (like) or left (pass) mechanism for quickly evaluating dating profiles on a smartphone. It gamifies dating and brings a new level of speed and superficiality to matchmaking that hadn't existed before. Tinder's approach becomes wildly popular, normalizing app-based dating and casual "swipe" judgments, and it significantly changes dating norms by making first impressions a predominantly digital (and appearance-driven) experience.

YEAR*	MILESTONE	NOTES
2012	Facebook Timeline & Life Curation	Facebook transitions user profiles to the Timeline format, encouraging people to fill in their life events from birth onward. Users begin curating not just current updates but their entire life story on social media. This change underscores the degree to which digital identity has matured: one's Facebook profile can now serve as a biographical scrapbook of their life, blending past and present, and it further blurs the boundary between one's online persona and real-life history.
2013	Snowden Revelations (NSA Spying)	Former NSA contractor Edward Snowden discloses classified documents revealing extensive global surveillance programs, including the collection of ordinary citizens' phone records, emails, and social media data. These revelations confirm many people's fears about government overreach in the digital age, severely eroding trust in governments and even tech companies (which unwittingly aided surveillance). The fallout boosts encryption use (more people adopting secure messaging, tech companies enabling end-to-end encryption) and sparks a worldwide debate on privacy vs. security in our networked lives.
2013	"Selfie" Culture	"Selfie" is declared the Word of the Year as self-photography dominates social feeds. Front-facing cameras on phones and apps like Instagram fuel this craze of snapping and sharing self-portraits. The selfie trend represents a new level of self-documentation and performance for peers online – people increasingly view everyday experiences in terms of shareable moments. One's image (literally) becomes a central part of online identity, and the trend also sparks discussions about vanity and the psychological effects of constant self-presentation.

YEAR*	MILESTONE	NOTES
2013	Carvana Launches Online Car Buying Platform	Carvana introduces a fully digital car-buying experience, allowing users to select, finance, and purchase vehicles without visiting a dealership. This marks a significant shift in consumer behavior, illustrating growing comfort with entrusting major life decisions to online platforms and visual representations alone.
2014	Slack	Slack enters workplace culture. It de-formalized communication (short, casual, emoji-laden), shifted workflows from email chains to perpetual open chatrooms, and blurred work-life boundaries ("always reachable"). It's a key milestone in digital presence bleeding into professional life.
2015	Ashley Madison Data Breach	Hackers steal and share the entire user database of Ashley Madison, a dating site for extramarital affairs. This exposes millions of real identities behind anonymous profiles, leading to public shaming, divorces, and even reported suicides. The breach vividly illustrates the stakes of privacy in the digital era: secrets kept in an online service can be made painfully public, and it underscores how much trust we place in platforms to safeguard our most sensitive personal information.
2015	Emoji	Oxford Dictionaries names an emoji ("Face with Tears of Joy" 😂) as the 2015 Word of the Year, recognizing the ubiquitous role of emojis in digital communication. People across cultures increasingly use these pictographs to convey emotion and tone in texts and social media, bridging gaps left by plain text. The rise of emoji as a quasi-universal language highlights how online communication norms evolve to help express personality and feelings when facial expressions and vocal tone are absent. We added to our alphabet.

You took a photo of your cup of Starbucks. Why not? Everyone else was posting snapshots like these of their daily lives. You added a caption, tapped the little "post" arrow, then waited. Likes came back. The feedback was a brand new kind of validation, unlike any you had felt before. You began curating your reality.

This was an explosive era. New technologies were emerging at a record pace. We were living differently. We still had the option of taking care of life's responsibilities on or offline. We could pay a bill by visiting a website or by writing a personal check and mailing it in. What's significant here is the number of us who chose the former.

Many of our leisure activities began migrating over to the digital world at this point. The video game industry, encompassing PC, console, and mobile gaming, began to outpace the motion picture industry in revenue. In 2013, for instance, the global video game industry generated approximately $70.4 billion, while the worldwide box office revenue for films was around $35.9 billion.

At this point, we could even buy a car online.

Arguably, the iPhone was the most influential innovation of this era. Without it, this book might not exist. Our phones were always with us. The web was no longer something we visited. It was something we were part of. Most of us were posting, swiping, scrolling, reacting, watching, gaming. We shared pieces of ourselves. I don't know about you, but I never reached for an outdated magazine in a waiting room again. My smartphone was all I needed to stay occupied.

Accessibility emerged. Voice-to-text, screen readers, and alt-text tools become reliable and widely integrated. These technologies increased digital access and usability for a broader range of users, expanding audienceship and reinforcing the internet as a shared, adaptive environment.

Barack Obama's presidential run was the first to fully integrate social media, including Facebook groups, YouTube videos, Twitter updates, and targeted ads, into its campaign strategy. The approach proved highly effective and has since become a standard feature of elections worldwide.

This was the time where identity took shape as something you had to manage. Some of it was fun, even empowering. Some of it was exhausting. Platforms gave us new ways to connect, but they also taught us to measure those connections in likes, shares, and followers, tasks done or undone, bills paid or unpaid.

We rarely stopped to think about it at the time. By the end of this stretch, digital life had woven itself into the background of everyday life, shaping not just what we did, but how we saw ourselves.

Fig. 12:4 The Architecture of Digital Transformation
2016 to 2020: Consciousness

tl;dr: Election interference, fake news, privacy breaches, and AI-driven content manipulation exposed unrealized vulnerabilities of digital platforms. Public skepticism of technology companies grew sharply. Digital presence became fraught with authenticity, security, and ethical concerns. At the same time, technology took huge strides, moving off our devices and into the world around us.

YEAR*	MILESTONE	NOTES
2016	Amazon Echo/Alexa	Normalizes having listening devices inside the home. Erosion of "private space" boundaries accelerates.
2016	Smart Appliances	Appliances such as refrigerators, washing machines, and ovens become connected to the internet, offering app-based controls and data monitoring.

YEAR*	MILESTONE	NOTES
2016	Google Translate	After many years of trying, Google switches from SMT to NMT, which uses deep learning to understand entire sentence context. This massively improves fluency, grammar, and meaning. Translation quality improves overnight. Users start trusting it for everyday use. Later, Chrome's built-in website translator also becomes reliably usable. Together, these two innovations break down language barriers.
2016	Pokémon Go	Pokémon Go debuts and instantly becomes a global craze, with players using their phone cameras and GPS to find and catch virtual creatures in real-world locations. It brings augmented reality to the masses, demonstrating a new form of play that overlays the digital onto the physical world. The sight of crowds roaming cities glued to their screens underscores both the exciting potential and odd social side effects of AR, raising safety/privacy issues (players trespassing, congregating in inappropriate places) and hinting at a future where digital and real spaces regularly intermingle.

YEAR*	MILESTONE	NOTES
2016	U.S. Election Interference	The 2016 U.S. presidential election becomes a showcase for online disinformation and foreign interference. Russian-backed entities run fake social media accounts and bots that spread divisive content and fake news to millions of Americans. This unprecedented cyber-campaign erodes confidence in social media as a force for good; it shows these platforms can be weaponized to sow discord and manipulate public opinion. In response, it prompts urgent discussions about safeguarding information integrity and the fragility of truth in the digital age.
2018	GDPR (General Data Protection Regulation)	First major global law asserting citizen rights over digital data is made. It sets strict rules for data collection, consent, access, portability, and erasure, and places legal responsibility on companies to protect user information. The regulation influences data privacy standards worldwide and marks a turning point in how governments approach digital rights.
2018	Cambridge Analytica Facebook Scandal	Political consulting firm Cambridge Analytica harvests data from tens of millions of Facebook users without consent and uses it to target voters. Public outrage erupts, prompting Facebook CEO Mark Zuckerberg's testimony to Congress. The incident is a watershed moment for data privacy awareness, showing how personal information on social media can be misused to manipulate opinions and erodes trust in Big Tech's stewardship of user data.

YEAR*	MILESTONE	NOTES
2018	Deepfake Awareness PSA	A viral video shows a convincing deepfake of President Obama (voiced by comedian Jordan Peele) delivering a message about fake news. This public service announcement, widely shared, brings mainstream attention to deepfake technology. It underscores the looming threat that anyone's likeness can be digitally forged, urging viewers to be skeptical of video content as authenticity can no longer be guaranteed.
2019	TikTok	TikTok (born from Musical.ly) explodes in popularity worldwide, especially among Gen Z. Its algorithm-driven feed of addictive short videos creates viral stars overnight and introduces new modes of creative expression (dances, challenges, memes). TikTok's rise shifts social media culture toward bite-sized, highly engaging content and raises new questions about algorithmic influence, data security (given its Chinese ownership), and the platform's impact on youth behavior and attention spans.
2020	COVID-19 And Remote Everything	The COVID-19 pandemic forces billions into lockdown and everyday life moves online. Offices turn to Zoom and Slack, schools adopt remote learning, and families socialize over video chats. This rapid digital pivot normalizes telepresence, demonstrating both the resilience of digital connectivity and the challenges (Zoom fatigue, isolation, blurred work-life boundaries) of sustaining human connection and identity when mediated entirely through screens.

You read or saw something that changed your mind. Then you found out it wasn't true. A photo, a quote, a comment. You thought Cindy Crawford looked surreal for her age, then you found out her bikini pics were photoshopped. She was still stunningly beautiful, but she looked real. Then, it was discovered that the so-called "original" was fake too. Altered to make Crawford look worse than she does in reality.

Shared, believed, then exposed. Trust wasn't broken in a moment. It was eroded, one pixel at a time.

By now, the benefits were undeniable. We could connect with friends instantly, build businesses from our phones, find community around almost anything. The convenience was real. So was the sense of possibility. These platforms expanded what a person could do, and in many ways, what a person could be. Breaches of trust exist across all eras, but this one was particularly defined by them.

On the other hand, innovation had shifted into high gear.

Language translation was paradigm-shifting. It evoked a return to pre-Tower-of-Babel Mesopotamia, a world where language no longer divided us. Whether speaking with someone in real time, reading foreign websites in Chrome, or using Google Translate, cross-language communication became unexpectedly fluid. The emergence of spoken language likely began in the Middle Paleolithic era, between 50,000 and 150,000 years ago, though some researchers argue it may date as far back as 1.5 million years. For the first time since speech itself began, a barrier that had separated cultures, communities, and content started to dissolve.

Home appliances and devices became increasingly "smart". Amazon Echo with Alexa enters widespread adoption, placing voice-controlled assistants into homes at scale for the first time. For many, digital presence had existed primarily through a keyboard or smartphone. Now, it was all around us.

More and more, scenarios began to present themselves where there was no offline option, no alternative, particularly during the pandemic.

There were also signs that not everything was as safe or stable as it seemed. Data breaches, surveillance programs, and manipulated content made headlines. We saw how easily trust could be stretched, and how quickly personal information could be exposed. Still, we kept going. It felt distant. Like hearing about a break-in down the street, but still sleeping with the windows open. The tools were too useful, too woven into daily life, to imagine doing without them.

Earlier, we talked about voting for your brother, who is hospitalized due to a skydiving accident. Imagine you go to the polls for him. At first, you easily complete the first few lines of the ballot. Then your mind goes blank. You can't remember what or who he wanted to vote for.

The term for that is *representational burden*. It is the acute awareness that fidelity, not personal preference, is your role. Proxy anxiety.

For some, that proxy anxiety had already begun to surface in the previous era. For most, it emerged here. I placed that line here, somewhat arbitrarily, because this is the pivot point where most of us had begun to exist in a digital dimension to a degree that made it a widespread phenomenon. A huge portion of the connected population crossed the proxy line in this era.

Somewhere outside our conscious awareness, we naturally began to feel a disconnection from the physical self. That self was somewhere else, like the hospitalized brother in the example, unable to respond in the present setting.

We couldn't identify it. We tried. Several of the most influential books on the topic were released in this era. As mentioned earlier, those texts were primarily focused on excess screen time, online bullying, and other dangers of the internet. All accurate, but they didn't tell the whole story.

Fig. 12:5 The Architecture of Digital Transformation
2021 to Present: Automation

tl;dr: Generative AI, deepfakes, and algorithmic content creation rapidly accelerate. NFTs, metaverse concepts, and AI-generated media shift digital life from documenting real experiences to fabricating new ones. The boundary between authentic and synthetic identity grows increasingly undetectable, while zero-UI living and post-device identity shape into reality.

YEAR*	MILESTONE	NOTES
2021	NFT Market and Digital Collectibles	Non-fungible tokens (NFTs), unique blockchain-based digital assets, explode in popularity. Digital art, clips, and virtual items sell for millions (e.g. Beeple's $69M NFT artwork), and a wave of celebrities and creators jump into the trend. The craze spotlights the concept of owning and flaunting digital goods as part of one's identity (using an NFT image as a profile picture to show membership or status). It also raises skepticism, as critics point out scams, speculative bubbles, and the environmental cost of blockchain transactions amid the euphoria for these new digital status symbols.
2021	Facebook Files Reveal Harms	Whistleblower Frances Haugen leaks internal Facebook documents ("Facebook Files") detailing how the company's platforms amplify toxic content and harm some users (e.g. Instagram's effect on teen girls), even as the company publicly downplayed these issues. The revelations confirm that social media can negatively shape mental health, self-image, and social divisions. This intensifies public outcry and regulatory interest, marking a turning point in how tech giants are held accountable for the societal impacts of their algorithms and design choices.

YEAR*	MILESTONE	NOTES
2022	Elon Musk's Twitter Takeover	Elon Musk acquires Twitter in a highly publicized, tumultuous deal that reshapes the platform's structure, governance, and public role. He removes moderation teams, overhauls verification, and reinstates previously banned accounts while publicly endorsing his own views on free speech and platform bias. The result is a sharp rise in impersonation, disinformation, and user confusion. Major advertisers withdraw, citing brand safety concerns. The takeover reveals how the personal ideology of a single owner can destabilize digital speech norms, erode institutional trust, and fragment what was once a central global platform.
2022	AI Image Generators	New AI tools like DALL·E 2, Midjourney, and Stable Diffusion allow users to create images from text prompts. Artists and the public marvel at AI's creative abilities, but the tools also spark controversy. They can be used to produce deepfake images or art in the style of living artists without consent. The advent of easy AI image generation blurs the line between human and machine creativity and raises fresh concerns about authenticity.
2022	ChatGPT	OpenAI releases ChatGPT, a remarkably human-like AI chatbot, to the public. Within days, it's generating essays, stories, and answers for over a million users, astonishing them with its fluidity. ChatGPT's viral success mainstreams the idea of AI as a conversational agent and content creator. Students experiment with it for homework, professionals for writing help. Its rise provokes both excitement and alarm: people realize AI can mimic human writing and knowledge convincingly, raising questions about the future of work (will AI automate certain jobs or tasks?), academic integrity, and the trustworthiness of content.

YEAR*	MILESTONE	NOTES
2022	Ruby Franke And Influencer Scandals	Family lifestyle branding collapses into criminal exposure and moral questioning.
2023	AI-Generated Media Hoaxes	Highly publicized incidents show AI's disruptive potential to fool the masses. In one case, an image of Pope Francis in a white Balmain coat (entirely AI-generated) goes viral, with many mistaking it for real. In another, an AI-simulated song imitating music stars Drake and The Weeknd racks up millions of streams before being taken down. These hoaxes demonstrate how convincingly AI can fabricate reality, underscoring a pressing challenge for society: developing skepticism, verification tools, and norms in a world where any photo, video, or audio can be faked with a few clicks.
2023	Hollywood Strikes Over AI Likeness	Hollywood screenwriters and actors go on strike, a key issue the use of AI to generate scripts and digital actors. Creatives demand protections against studios using AI to replicate their writing style or their likeness without fair compensation. This labor dispute highlights a broader societal concern: people are fighting to retain control over their creative output and personal identity in the face of rapidly improving AI.
2025	Majorana 1 Quantum Chip	Microsoft unveils quantum chip advancement, to mixed reactions; raising hopes for breakthroughs and fears over destabilizing cybersecurity.
2025	AI Governance Platforms Emerge	Early frameworks for AI oversight emerge, struggling to keep pace with technology and revealing gaps in ethical control.
2025	Duolingo Replaces Developers with AI	Duolingo announces that generative AI is now creating language-learning content more effectively than its own staff. The company restructures around AI-led instruction, demonstrating that machine-designed education can outperform traditional methods at scale.

*Years are approximate.

By now, digital life wasn't an add-on. It became the environment. The pandemic only cemented what was already true for many of us. We *had to* work, shop, bank, read, relax, and socialize online. From leisure to business to personal errands, a large part of our lives was, and is, already digital. And we preferred it that way.

In that context, the arrival of deepfakes, generative AI, and synthetic content represented a shift in one part of our digital lives, while much of the rest remained unchanged. The average person saw it as just another development in an already fast-moving digital world. The media framed it as a threat. Teachers struggled to know whether a term paper was written by a student or by AI.

NEXT

In the not-too-distant future, we'll likely see ambient sensing ecosystems, where your thermostat knows your mood based on conditions like fog or sunshine. Cars and wearables have already begun detecting signs of anxiety, emergency, or illness. That could feasibly be expanded to include even moral distress, or pulse quickening, prompting changes in our environment or behavior.

Ovens are available now that scan a QR code and automatically set themselves to the right times and temperatures to cook the food inside.

Ambient Intelligence (AmI) and Zero User Interface (UI) are also quickly approaching, where little or no interaction is needed at all. Your phone, watch, speaker, glasses, or home will be activated by gesture, voice, biometrics, or predictive behavior. It will make logging in obsolete and opting out nearly impossible.

Business Insider recently ran an article entitled "CEOs who aren't yet preparing for the quantum revolution are 'already too late,' IBM exec says. I'd like to qualify that statement to mean companies with specific, complex problems that can be addressed by quantum computing. The article goes on to say that the practical use of quantum computing will depend also on AI. Still, using a hybrid approach that leverages quantum computing and AI, we can expect major shifts in delivery route optimization, inventory management and supply chain resilience.

Similarly, the way goods are produced is undergoing the largest shift since the industrial revolution. Some speculate that the era we're currently in will be looked back upon in the future as the "automation revolution". Vision systems can detect a range of issues, trends and behaviors, then talk to machinery like robotic arms to change the way the production line operates in response, or if it operates at all, in the case of defective product.

The Drug Supply Chain Security Act (DSCSA) was signed into law on November 27, 2013 by President Barack Obama, as part of the broader Drug Quality and Security Act (DQSA). It required pharmaceutical companies to use an interoperable, electronic system to identify and trace prescription drugs as they are distributed in the United States. The goal was to prevent counterfeit, stolen, contaminated, or otherwise harmful drugs from reaching patients.

The implementation of the DSCSA influenced pharmaceutical manufacturers to adopt advanced vision systems. To meet serialization and traceability requirements, high-speed inspection technologies were added to production lines. These vision systems use high-resolution cameras and image recognition software to read barcodes, lot numbers, and expiration dates with precision. They are there to make sure every package is accurate, and every shipment can be traced.

As expectations for real-time data have increased, artificial intelligence and machine learning have become part of the process. These tools can now detect printing errors, verify package labels, and spot inconsistencies before products leave the facility. This reduces the risk of noncompliance and increases operational efficiency.

Imagine a conveyor belt in a factory where bottles of Gatorade are moving at a rate of anywhere between 6 to 20 bottles per second. The human eye will detect a blur of movement. The type of high-resolution camera used in applications like these can not only detect the bottle and its details. It can actually detect accuracy down to ensuring that all the seals on the cap are intact. If any are broken, it triggers a response that will re-route the bottle to a rejects pile, or activate a robotic arm to push it off the assembly line. All in a portion of a second.

At this point, industrial AI is just crossing the threshold where vision systems like these begin to be a practical option for manufacturers at a larger scale. In the not-too-distant future, quality control will largely be performed by these systems. The best part, it's accurate, to say that this type of high-speed machine vision technology does not eliminate jobs (a vital and often-misunderstood point).

No human worker can inspect individual bottle caps, barcodes, or seals at that pace, let alone detect minute defects in real time. Instead of eliminating human labor, the technology shifts it. It takes over tasks that were never feasible for humans to do manually, freeing people to handle higher-order decision-making, like assembly line oversight, and maintenance. At the same time, it makes nearly every product that hits a store shelf safer and exponentially reduces defects.

AI agents are being developed that can respond to messages, manage content, and make choices on your behalf, drawing from your past behavior to stand in for your present self.

The next step will be digital twins: AI-driven representations of you that may attend meetings or train in professional or educational environments.

Advancements in Extended Reality (XR), encompassing AR, VR, and MR, are creating immersive environments that enhance training, collaboration, and entertainment. These technologies are increasingly integrated with AI to provide adaptive and context-aware experiences. They will reshape learning. Imagine being able to ask questions of an entity that has endless answers, to have a virtual instructor sense the pace at which you need to learn. It has already been proven that AI greatly facilitates learning. We can expect that trajectory to continue.

Similarly, the development of holographic interfaces, supported by 6G networks and integrated sensing, is enabling real-time, three-dimensional representations of people and objects. This leap forward facilitates more natural and engaging remote interactions, transforming fields such as telemedicine, education, and virtual meetings.

A friend recently asked ChatGPT to write an obituary for an elderly relative who had passed away. At the service, the priest gushed more than once, "Honestly, this is one of the best obituaries I've seen in a long time." She wasn't sure how to respond. Does she take credit, or doesn't she?

We don't know yet.

CHAPTER THIRTEEN

Selves Gone Rogue

DECISIONS MADE FOR YOU

Duality does not always feel chaotic. Sometimes, it feels organized. Managed. Even admired. But if the parts are no longer speaking to each other, some coherence has been lost.

An acquaintance of mine, we'll call him George, has an Amazon subscription for his favorite coffee beans. They're grown in Jamaica, and you can't find them in stores here. Two new bags of beans are delivered to his doorstep every 30 days.

That's not new. Mail order has been around for a long time. The degree to which it is automated now does make a difference. Unless George logs in and says he doesn't want his coffee this month, a UPS label will automatically print out somewhere in a fulfillment warehouse with his address on it. George's proxy. But that's not what makes his story notable.

Up to that point, the coffee would arrive on his doorstep right when he needed it. Until one month, George told me, there was something wrong with the delivery. Whether it got lost in transit, sank to the bottom of the ocean, or someone in Amazon's warehouse was enjoying a really good cup of joe that day, George didn't know. Amazon didn't offer a reason, only that the box was not coming.

Here's where things get recursive. A day or so later, George was issued a refund. A virtual "George" made a decision for George. The autonomy was deferred to an automated task without his permission. Maybe George would have rather had them re-ship the coffee. The decision was made by proxy.

Passive participation.

Your bank automatically transferring funds from one account to another to avoid overdraft may be an example, if you didn't explicitly grant them permission to do so.

Your printer refusing to print using toner you bought when it reaches a level it deems "low enough to stop". Personally, I've always been suspicious of that warning that it's "unsafe" to keep printing, but I could be wrong.

Maybe you're driving in a rental car, and it has an auto feature your car doesn't. So, unbeknownst to you, it responds to everyone who texts you while you're in the care that you're "driving now and will call them later." When you arrive, you're greeted by an irritated group, and you're honestly clueless. A virtual "you" had made a decision you didn't agree with (although we really shouldn't text while we drive).

You request a ride, through a rideshare app. The route isn't the best, but you didn't get a choice. You paid for the extra mile or two, and it took you longer to get there.

You're freezing, but your thermostat thinks nobody's home, so it just turned off the heat.

In a high-stakes example, in 2022, a Tesla Model 3 driver was forced by Autopilot back into original the lane after attempting to merge around stopped traffic. The system perceived the merge as unsafe, even though it was intentional. The car corrected course and collided with the stopped vehicle. The driver said the system "overruled" their evasive maneuver.

These scenarios illustrate what digital duality can become when left uncalibrated. They're proxy decisions that are in conflict with human awareness, your awareness.

DECISIONS MADE BY YOU

Sometimes we choose the uncalibrated state on our own. That shift can happen gradually, even consciously. Let's take a look at two real Reddit threads. They both demonstrate what it feels like to be close to someone whose digital self has eclipsed their physical presence.

The posts appear here as originally written. Spelling and grammar have not been corrected.

In this post, in the /TrueOffMyChest subreddit, an anonymous user (throwaway84112788221), recounts visiting their brother and his new wife, who is an active Instagram influencer.

"My Brother's Wife Is an Influencer and I Can't Believe How Exhausting It Is"

"This week was the first time meeting my sister-in-law in person. I'm in the armed forces and between me not being stationed near family, the pandemic and overseas service I have never met her in person. (Though we have done video calls, chatted on the phone and sent messages). I was sent overseas and could not attend the wedding. I was able to watch a live stream through.

I don't have any social media and I rarely look at what anyone else is posting. My sister-in-law is very active on instagram because she's an influencer. I had no idea it was so time consuming and exhausting.

For instance her and my brother filmed and took photos of Christmas day weeks ago. She is only posting them now. It's because she wants her followers to see a certain aesthetic. If she didn't tell me they were taken weeks ago I would have never guessed. **I found out they live in the basement of their house for everyday life because the main floor (kitchen, living room, bedroom etc) are for filming.** I just thought they had a clean house. I wondered because everything in the house is white from the photos my brother sent me. Now I understand.

My parents have a farm and my sister-in-law and brother have spent hours filming video and taking photos in the woods out back. It's so my sister-in-law can post them later on and say they went on a vacation to a cabin in the woods. (Note that there is no cabin here. The cabin they'll use in the pictures is from another time)

I think it was strange that she spent time doing her hair and makeup and getting herself and my brother dressed up for all that but to each their own. I also found out that they had their wedding sponsored and people at the wedding had to agree to be filmed or be in ads. I know my parents have been on her instagram a few times. I don't want to be on her social media so I said I can't because of the armed forces. She has never posted anything about me or mentioned anything. I know it is a lie but it keeps the peace.

I just can't believe how time consuming and exhausting it all is. My sister-in-law seems nice. I have no problems with her and if her and my brother want to do all that for her instagram it's their life. I couldn't do it though. She spends so much time on instagram when she isn't taking photos or video."

We don't want to lose one life to gain another. Sadly, this couple seems to have done just that. There is no mention of children here, but if they do start a family, their kids' perspectives could look a lot like this other, well-known, Reddit post, in the same sub, by user AnnonymousCarrot, who was 16 at the time:

"My mom is an influencer and I hate her for it"

"-long post- My mom (f45) has become a facebook influencer, I (f16) used to not care when she took photos but its gotten crazy. Everything she does is now posted or live streamed online. Even if somewhere says don't photograph or film she'd find a way to film it. It was annoying at first but now its downright frustrating especially since 3 months ago when she got really into it. I also completely understand the irony of me posting this on Reddit but I just need someone to hear me out.

I declined my 16th birthday party so she threw a giant party claiming it was for her anniversary, my brothers graduation, and my birthday. There were 150 guests and between my dad, my brother and myself we only covered 30 of them. I don't even know how much of that party she wasn't on her screen for since she was constantly filming and uploading it, along with a lot of her friends. I really wanted to preform there, i practiced for months but the idea of her filming and uploading it made me so nervous i backed down. I don't like being photographed or filmed, even as a kid I didn't.

Another time we went on vacation and every second it was filmed. When we got to a hotel we weren't allowed in until she recorded the room even if we just drove for 8 hours and wanted to sleep. She'd take her time in areas she could photograph even if it was a rock (actual thing), but when me, my dad and brother tried to enjoy a non-aesthetic place I felt rushed like she wanted to just go. If we got food she didn't let us eat or move the food until photos and videos were taken, even having us pose with the food or announce what it is. That one annoyed me. One time we traveled by car and it was over 10 hours since we ate. When we got a chance to eat dinner she took my food before I got a chance and was recording it saying things like "oooh how delicious," and i was so tired and hungry I just gave up and started tearing up.

On the vacation when we went on a boat but she was live streaming, she was calling out followers thanking them and saying how much she loved them all. The boat was going to check out Alcatraz and I thought it was so disrespectful especially because it was a public area and not everyone wants to be filmed, and also the history of the island makes me feel that it needs to be respected and not treated as a background to a video.

One thing that made me want to write this post was because I was trying to get a drink out of the soda machine, she had me pour out the ice from the cup so she could record me doing it for a shot. I have a certain ice to soda ratio I like and it was perfect the first time. After that I didn't get it correct and it was just a damper on an already not so great day. After that she held up my soda and was showing it off to the camera and I had to just wait until she was done.

Another thing is I've started to envy her followers. She gives them so much more attention then me. She goes off on my dad about how much closer I am with him than her, but I asked to watch a movie with her and she declines. Her reasoning is always that she has a livestream later shes hosting, or a video to film, or her followers are live. Shes turned me down so many times I stopped even trying to hangout with her, since if i do get her around shes on her phone. One time I asked for her opinion and she snapped that she was tired from her job, and that she needed time to post. She livestreams so much that I sometimes have to skip meals *because she cant have the background noise and she livestreams in the middle of the kitchen. Shes live streams for hours and if she had any issue with the internet she makes everyone power down their devices so she can get a better connection.*

The most attention she's given me recently was recorded, I was in a dance class and the only time she looked at me was when she was recording what I was doing. The instructor praised me to them for my work multiple times and she didn't even notice, I checked and she was watching a livestream.

I feel like I'm going crazy, when she posts about me I feel exposed like I have no control. My dad keeps saying she views the world through lens and I have no clue if this is how parents are now a days but its terrible, I'm so sorry if anyone else has to grow up like this."

Some people stay entrenched in their digital persona, too focused on narrating everything from outside themselves, but rarely being present in the room or for the people they love. To those around them, the influencer begins to like a brand ambassador for their own life. They appear to be thinking of every moment as content. The bigger picture becomes the only picture. And slowly, something shifts. In these Reddit posts, you can feel the sense of loss the writers express. There is far less duality. The person appears to have chosen their virtual life over their physical one.

These two are extreme examples. The reality is, this doesn't just happen to people trying to build large followings, and it's usually not as extreme.

In subtler way, you might find yourself rehearsing how you'll describe a moment before you've actually lived it. You might be in a conversation while also observing how it will look if quoted, shared, or saved. You might be composing instead of connecting.

For example, a mother follows her toddler across the play structure with her phone in hand. Every few minutes, she crouches to take a photo or a short video. The memory being captured has replaced the moment being lived.

You can't make your way through a crowd to view a historic monument. There are too many people there, paused for too long, to capture just the right selfie with the monument in the background.

Or maybe it's just something simple, like scrolling on our phone while with others in a restaurant, or staying indoors gaming on a beautiful day.

If we're honest, most of us have been guilty of this at one point or another. We have allowed our digital presence to take over, becoming uncalibrated.

OPPOSITION IS PARTICIPATION

The same can be true in reverse.

To gain perspective, for me personally, this was low-hanging-fruit. All I needed to do was pay a visit to Uncle Henley.

Henley didn't disappoint. I sat down. He wanted to know how he could help, so I started explaining, in the most general terms, what I was researching and why. I might have talked for about a second-and-a-half. I don't think the entire word "digital" had even crossed my lips when he cut me off -

"I'm not online."

I knew this. Everyone in my family knows it. Uncle Henley says it often, with faint note of superiority. As if that fact alone grants him moral distance from everyone else. He doesn't say it out loud, but the implication is that we're all "weak suckers who are getting pulled in". I should add that Uncle Henley is not elderly. It isn't the *inability* to use a computer that makes him like this.

He sees headlines and claims to understand the culture. He has a GoodRx card, and my cousin books his flights for him online, with him peering over her shoulder as she types. But he doesn't follow, and he's not ashamed of that in the least. He has an EZ Pass transponder in his car that pays tolls for him as he drives.

What he believes is moral superiority is, sorry to say, really ignorance. Don't worry, his name has been changed. Not that he would read this anyway.

Say a reference comes up at the family Thanksgiving. Everyone laughs, except him. He smiles politely but doesn't ask. He's proud of not knowing. He's built an identity out of not being "pulled in."

He doesn't realize that refusing to have a smart thermostat still means relying on a digital utility grid. A flip phone is still connected. The traffic on the roads he drives on is calibrated and timed by algorithms, the products he buys have been manufactured and delivered to the he shops using repeated means of automation throughout the entire process, and he has Hulu.

Uncle Henley mirrors the influencer who needs to be seen. This man needs *not* to be seen, to protect a worldview that he feels is under threat. He's ignoring a side of him that exists, whether he likes it or not.

If he ever does decide to try, it will be with such an underdeveloped sense of digital self that he will likely be easily manipulated by the everyday hoaxes most of us scroll right past.

He's also the first to likely experience the effects of unconscious duality, because he's the most unaware in general.

These people are far more integrated than they think.

Opposition is not the opposite of participation. It is one of its forms. A system becomes durable when it can contain its critics, when it can make resistance useful to its own calibration. Henley's withdrawal is not immunity. It is data.

The goal is to stay with what is unfolding while still understanding what it's part of. To hold the "we" while still being fully "I." Not to choose between the digital and physical realms, but to be aware that you exist in both at once.

PART III

PROXY MANAGEMENT

CHAPTER FOURTEEN
Seeing the Cost in Free

IN CONTEXT

Looking at the divide from different perspectives helped me to recognize our own part in the process.

At the corporate level, structured questioning looks a certain way, depending on your role.

As a techie, I was focused on the backend, the coding and the architecture. What defines an effective tool? People who work in that realm will tell you, it's exceptionally rare to find a developer who can connect what is built with real human wants and needs. Nobody really knows why. Maybe they're asking the wrong questions, too.

As an IT Director, I was responsible for focusing on what is measurable, and what is not; data analytics versus corporate branding strategy.

Labor relations gave me "soft" positives, like awareness and image, and intangible, unmeasurable facts. It also taught me a lot about persuasion tactics coming from both sides.

It gave me a limited background in law, which I noticed can be set in stone, or interpretive. That contextual reasoning is something AI is incapable of.

As a content creator, engagement was my benchmark for success. Traffic, clicks, visits, likes, impressions and engagement are the only goals here.

Throughout this entire career progression of mine, I was also a user. Like you, I've defined my own preferences.

Macro: Which smartphone I prefer, the apps I use, the devices I have in my home.

And micro, which tends to be far more impulsive: who I accept as a connection or friend, what and when I post. Whether I tag or untag myself. What I use the tools for. Do I text or call, this time? Is Alexa just a kitchen timer? Do I use AI in creative ways? What's a permanent vs. a temporary chat?

The various roles did help to make things clearer.

We're the end point. Until we aren't.

HOW CAN RECURSION EXIST IF IT ISN'T RECURSIVE?

If systems are designed to be recursive, and recursion is a loop, then how can there be an end point? How can this be a trap?

This question comes up a lot. To understand why some data vanishes and some evolves into influence, consider this.

Literally every program ever written was designed for us. Humans. AI exists for *us*. It is not an origin, and it is not a destination. It is a function that only resolves when called. AI systems are framed as autonomous but only resolve meaningfully in response to human interaction.

Just about everyone who ever took a programming class has, in the back of their closet, an old, out-of-date laptop collecting dust. It's unlikely they will ever spend the ten minutes it would take to boot the thing up again.

Residing on that laptop's hard drive is a program they wrote to pass that class.

A mini application, shaped by late-night, Mountain Dew-fueled logic and deadlines. Nothing important or groundbreaking, just proof the student had acquired the technical skills to develop it.

The program ran, returned whatever output it was supposed to, they got their course grade, and everyone moved on.

Let's assume that program will never be run again. It didn't fail. It was just never retrieved after the class ended. It reached its end.

Recursion is contingent upon use. A loop only loops if someone runs it. In digital culture, we're trained to imagine systems as ever-on, evolving independently of us.

What application or service trains us to believe this? Is it Microsoft? Google? TikTok? An Amazon Echo Show? Universities?

The answer is every one of them. Remember, everything you call and receive output from is recursive by design. That recursion is what makes them useful and effective. The creators only profit when we believe they're self-sustaining, and that *we're* the ones who must catch up.

So, a notification pops up, and we input once again. It's easy to assume the machine keeps learning. The platform keeps adapting. The algorithm keeps running.

But if no one asks a question, nothing gets returned. The loop ends.

The idea that these systems evolve on their own is part of the illusion. They don't. When we stop showing up, they break. Tumblr's algorithm stalled when users left in droves after the 2018 content bans. Facebook quietly downgraded its News tab after attention moved elsewhere. These platforms didn't function the way they were trained to, because their only engine was us, and we didn't engage in the way they predicted we would.

A lack of awareness of our role in choice conditioning can cost us.

ACCEPTING DUALITY IN ACCESS TO INFORMATION

Having unlimited information makes us smarter, more informed, and more rational. It also dumbs us down with mindless scrolling and low-quality content. The internet is an important part of our lives. People also get scammed there, and lose themselves there.

When the internet was new, we had people who embraced it, and others who actively hated it. Now, we need to accept both views so we can mentally prepare ourselves for whatever comes next.

RETHINKING CLOSENESS AND CONNECTION

Being always connected via texts, social media, and video calls can build deeper relationships. It can deepen bonds, reconnect old friends, or allow us to witness life moments we'd otherwise miss. But it can also enable access for bad actors when we feel alone, bored, or off-guard.

It's like being in a huge crowd. You couldn't possibly make the judgment that everyone in that crowd was good or bad. The internet is too big a place for us to place a single label on. It is both.

SEEING THE COST IN FREE

Appreciating the richness that our favorite platforms add to our lives, while never overlooking their business models. **There is a cost to data surveillance.** That cost is time and attention, behavior and identity-shaping. We are conditioned by the choices we make.

The cost is not always monetary. While platforms often present themselves as free, the economic cost is simply displaced. It is hidden behind personalization, convenience, and habit. Here, we'll explore some of these. The examples provided are not intended to single out a particular company, they're just there to help clarify the description.

MONETARY COST

These are costs that appear indirect or invisible, yet result in financial outlay or economic manipulation.

Data-exchange Pricing (Google, Facebook)

Your personal data is bartered invisibly for access and exposure. The platform feels free, but your identity is sold again and again.

Behavioral Spending Nudges (Amazon, Instagram, TikTok)

What feels like spontaneous desire is often manufactured through targeting. You end up buying things you didn't plan to want.

Freemium Traps and Subscriptions (Spotify, Apple, YouTube)

Free tiers are psychologically engineered to be uncomfortable. You pay not just for better service, but for relief from friction, usually in the form of annoying ads or a limit on features you can access.

Clickbait and Misinformation Traps (YouTube, TikTok, Online Ads)

Sensational content and emotional bait are engineered to maximize clicks. Some links conceal malware or scams. Others deliver misinformation that leads to costly real-world consequences.

Ecosystem Entrapment (Apple, Amazon Prime)

The platform builds a closed-loop ecosystem of services, hardware, and perks. You use your iPhone, iCloud, Apple Music, Apple TV+, App Store, and maybe AppleCare. The services feel like part of one elegant whole. But each is billed separately, often monthly, and some are subtly necessary to keep the ecosystem functional (e.g., iCloud for backups). It becomes your default, and not necessarily because it's cheaper, or better.

COGNITIVE COST

The way systems take their toll on us, mentally, is a very different kind of cost, arguably a higher-value one than monetary cost. One that affects perception, critical thinking, and mental autonomy.

Predictive steering (Google)

Your intentions are shaped before you're fully aware of them. What begins as choice becomes subtly predetermined.

Perception (YouTube)

Your understanding of reality is shaped by algorithmic exposure rather than direct experience. What you see becomes what you believe.

Independent thought (Reddit)

Group norms and community validation replace self-directed inquiry. Popularity (upvoting) substitutes for truth.

Attention (Netflix)

Your cognitive bandwidth is depleted by passive, continuous engagement. The platform encourages immersion without reflection.

Skim Culture (Most platforms)

Our tendency to skim quickly, rather than absorb content at the same speed as having a conversation or reading a book erodes our attention span.

The journalist and writer Nicholas Carr echoes this in his warnings about how digital environments degrade contemplative thought.

According to Carr, the faster our minds move across surfaces, the less likely we are to stop and examine the structure beneath them. Recursive logic makes information feel like intelligence. But feeling smart is not the same as thinking clearly.

BEHAVIORAL COST

This category includes subtle design choices that nudge users toward specific behaviors that influence habit formation, decision-making, and routine actions. You are being pre-primed to spend, click, or commit before you're even consciously aware of making a decision. This cost is incurred not through deliberate coercion, but by engineering in behavioral defaults that align with platform goals rather than your own.

Desire (Amazon)

Your wants are engineered before you are consciously aware of them.

Optionality (Apple)

Your behavioral choices are narrowed invisibly through walled ecosystems.

Emotional Autonomy (Spotify)

Your mood and internal state are influenced externally by patterns of consumption.

Compulsion (Free Games, e.g. Candy Crush Saga)

Play is framed as harmless, but the design subtly manipulates urgency and reward. Levels are artificially difficult, progress is throttled, and optional payments are framed as shortcuts, but they're really necessary to progress. The cost is compulsion. You're nudged into micro-spending through manufactured friction that exploits your persistence.

Commitment Streaks (Snapchat, Duolingo)

Daily streaks and rewards reframe voluntary engagement as obligation. Users return not because they want to, but because they don't want to break a chain, or miss a reward. The cost is commitment. Your motivation shifts from internal curiosity to external continuity enforcement.

Frictionless Agreement (Default Opt-ins, Cookies, Permissions)

By structuring choices to favor passive acceptance, platforms normalize consent without users fully understanding the parameters. Few read privacy agreements. Most just check "I agree" boxes because they know they can't continue unless they do. The cost is discernment.

PSYCHOSOCIAL COST

These are costs that intersect where mental health, social connection, and identity meet. They include the loss of self-worth from constant comparison on social media, the shaping of identity by repeated exposure to narrow content, and the weakening of real relationships as digital interactions replace face-to-face ones. Psychosocial costs may not be immediately visible, but over time they influence how people feel about themselves, how they relate to others, and how they build a sense of belonging.

Individuality as a Negative Trait (TikTok)

Personal uniqueness is discouraged through aesthetic mimicry and trend conformity.

Self-worth (Instagram)

Value and popularity are externally determined by metrics of visibility and comparison.

Trust (Facebook)

Social bonds are filtered through monetized engagement, eroding genuine connection.

Relational Erosion (YouTube, TikTok, Facebook)

Time spent in curated feeds displaces presence in real-world relationships. You share less, scroll more, and feel connected less.

Identity Formation (All platforms)

Repeated exposure to narrow types of content influences how you see yourself. Over time, identity becomes shaped by consumption patterns instead of values, relationships, or real-world experiences.

ABILITY TO ENGAGE AT BOTH THE META AND MICRO LEVEL SIMULTANEOUSLY

We may be dual, but at the same time, we're still one, cranially. Our nervous system didn't evolve to manage dual selves.

Authenticity now means there is an alignment of our two personas. It's an alignment we will need, in order to maintain balance, during all of our waking hours.

Everything we do, say, post, livestream, and react to, will now be viewed through a new lens. Those who are early adopters of this new viewpoint will feel more grounded and stable in this new, dual existence of ours. The alternative seems to be to feel fragmented and not know why.

Fig. 14:1 Hidden Costs

How popular platforms reshape behavior, identity, and attention while appearing free.

PLATFORM	MECHANISM + HIDDEN COST
Google	Indexes every curiosity and turns search history into behavioral prediction. The cost is autonomy. Your intentions are shaped by what you are shown next.
Amazon	Reinforces consumption habits through frictionless convenience and personalized nudges. The cost is desire. You begin to want what has already been selected for you.
Apple	Curates your digital environment through hardware, app gatekeeping, and subtle design choices. The cost is optionality. Your choices narrow without your awareness.
YouTube	Guides your viewing toward algorithmic reinforcement of belief, identity, and familiarity. The cost is perception. What you consume begins to define what you think.
TikTok	Captures attention through rapid emotional loops and visual mimicry. The cost is individuality. You scroll into sameness without realizing it.
Facebook	Optimizes engagement through emotional triggers and filtered connection. The cost is trust. Relationships are mediated through conflict and affirmation.
Instagram	Elevates aesthetic comparison and curates performance as identity. The cost is self-worth. Value is assigned by visibility.
Reddit	Creates group belonging through consensus, karma, and niche immersion. The cost is independent thought. Community coherence replaces complexity.
Spotify	Reinforces mood states and identity markers through curated playlists. The cost is emotional autonomy. Your inner landscape becomes externally managed.
Netflix	Encourages passive entertainment through infinite scroll and auto-play. The cost is attention. Reflection is replaced by narrative sedation.

ASKING THE RIGHT QUESTIONS

"You only think I don't know where the poison is, because I know you know I know you know..."

- Vizzini, The Princess Bride

In this classic bit of comedic brilliance, Vizzini asks question after question, each based on the previous wrong assumption, until he finally outsmarts himself. And it's a perfect example of how recursive logic doesn't uncover truth. It buries it. In the movie, he ends up confidently picking up the wrong vial and drinking the poison.

A question can expand thought, engage another person in conversation, or it can send you down a spiraling rabbit hole. Some people simply don't ask enough questions, which can make them appear shy, arrogant, indifferent, or inattentive. Or, maybe they just don't want to sound like Vizzini.

The biggest misconceptions about digital duality evolved from asking the wrong questions. Here, we'll explore some common logical fallacies that enabled even experts to develop erroneous theories about digitality and society. Examples include assumptions we've made about the digital world, based on questions that fall into well-known categories of logical fallacies:

Framing Fallacy

Misleading phrasing: "Why can't I focus?"

The fallacy: When a question is shaped in a way that limits the possible answers, often excluding more accurate or meaningful interpretations.

The issue: This line of questioning frames it as a personal failure of attention, rather than as a shift in how attention is distributed across dual selves, conditions that affect everyone. The answers might be "fatigue", "burnout" or "personal weakness". The problem isn't that we're tired. It's that we're fragmented and trying to operate as one. If we limit the possible answers to internal traits, we exclude environmental causes.

Insight-producing questioning: "When did I start to feel unfocused? What changed in my environment that might have been a root cause?"

False Cause (Post Hoc Ergo Propter Hoc)

Misleading phrasing: "Smartphones caused a rise in ADHD," or "young people today are illiterate because of too much screen time."

The fallacy: Assuming that because one thing follows another, it must be the cause.

The issue: Questions like these commit a post hoc fallacy by attributing a complex, multi-variable outcome (changes in reading behavior, comprehension, expression, etc.) to a single, convenient culprit (screens or technology). It also reflects cultural bias disguised as diagnosis.

Insight-producing questioning: "How has the structure of modern attention changed," or "Are we mistaking divided presence for damaged attention?"

False Dichotomy

Misleading phrasing: "Either we resist technology or robots and AI will take all of our jobs."

The fallacy: Presenting only two options when more exist.

The issue: This flattens the conversation and skips over the much more subtle, ongoing reality of living across both analog and digital selves without fully understanding either. Questions like "At what point will AI surpass us?" or "Will robots take our jobs?" ignore the fact that this is an environment we're already in. Our current digital state is one where optimism and fear happen at the same time, often when discussing the same topic. The illusion of a future crisis delays recognition of present conditions. Now is the only time we have the option to play a role in shaping the trajectory.

Insight-producing questioning: "How do we navigate this?" and "Accepting the realities, what is our desired goal, and how will we achieve that goal?"

Choice Conditioning
noun
/ˈchois kən-ˈdi-sh(ə-)niŋ/

A process by which the system structures perceived options in advance of decision-making. Rather than making choices freely, users select from paths shaped by prior engagement, platform incentives, and algorithmic guidance.

Circular Reasoning (Begging the Question)

Misleading phrasing: "Is my kid wasting too much time on social media?"

The fallacy: Using an assumption as proof of the conclusion.

The issue: Time management feels like an unachievable goal for you. This assumes the problem is a lack of personal control, and that more optimization will solve it. You are not overwhelmed because you've made bad choices. You're overwhelmed because choice is no longer the primary mechanism shaping your experience.

Insight-producing questioning: "Why has time become something I feel I must manage at all times? Who or what made it feel scarce?" or "When did being 'on top of things' become the baseline expectation, and who benefits from that belief?"

Each of these shifts the focus from a failing of self-discipline to a more complex mix of personal choices and systemic structure, from choice-making to choice-conditioning.

CHAPTER FIFTEEN
You Are Here, But Also There

SPLIT ACROSS SPACE AND SCREEN

We used to follow time. Now we sync to its fragments.

Time still dictates pace: sunrises, seasons, schedules, routines.

Back in the day, the postal service, and the manual way everything operated, used to as well. There was a culturally-pervasive expectation that waiting was inevitable. If you had to write an essay, you'd go to the library. Now, it can be due tomorrow because you have instant access to twelve sources without leaving your couch.

There was a sense of order, presence, even a kind of safety. There was a rhythm to life that kept people more grounded, even when they were in a hurry.

The pace was comfortable, and shared. It was part of the design.

Time is no longer whole. It no longer unfolds in linear rhythm. Instead, it's broken into push alerts, short-form content, task switching, algorithmic nudges. At the same time, it is interrupted by what is going on in the physical room; conversation, ambient sound, hunger, fatigue. Two presences. One clock. Endless dissonance.

Decades ago, jarring, out-of-context moments were less frequent. You received one letter. One daily newspaper delivered to your driveway. One phone call. Now, these messages are consistent. We receive hundreds per day, absorbed as fragments (which they usually are). If jarring, out-of-context moments have always created a certain emotional dissonance in the moment they are experienced, imagine what the average person is putting themselves through on an hourly basis.

The magnitude of this shift, and its effects, are only beginning to be understood. It has radically altered how we perceive time, and how we spend our day. The fact that your digital self never sleeps has further realigned time for much of the human race in unprecedented ways. Those parts of your digital self that speak without your permission update even when you're quiet. They exist in time, but in a very different way.

Fig. 15:1 Parallel Presence: An Everyday Comparison
A snapshot of how we *feel* time across environments in our daily life, as digital life accelerates and decelerates, while physical time holds steadier rhythms.

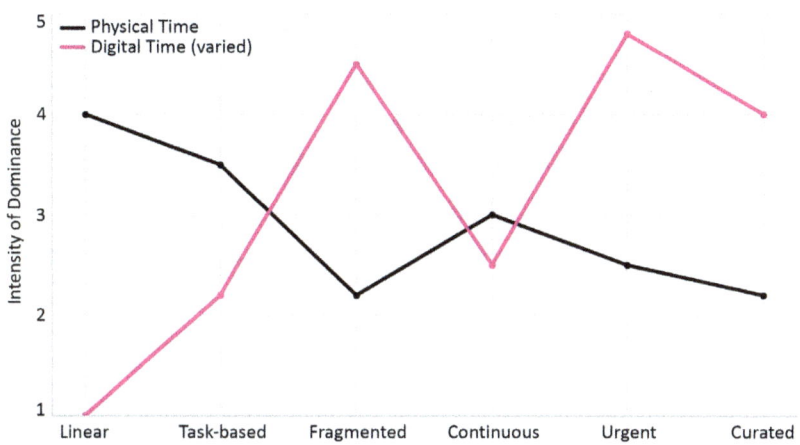

This is how parallel presence looks, temporally. We have two timelines now; we are living in *parallel* time. That can make it seem like time is passing more quickly. If that's the case, the dissonance you may feel is a split in presence.

THE CHRONOPHORIC SPLIT

Human time is existential time. It is created by the astronomical rhythms of the cosmos; solar rotation, planetary orbit, lunar phases. We live briefly, within this physical structure of time, and we perceive it through change.

Memory accumulates, intention unfolds, and presence is metabolized through awareness. Human time is felt as linear, irreversible, and embodied. It is sequenced through limitation, aging, and decay. You are in time because you are alive within it.

Digital time is synthetic. Instead of being lived, it's referenced and indexed.

Say there are two files created on the same date. Today's date. Two centuries from now, for the first time since they were saved and stored, someone needs data from one of the files.

The files themselves are ageless. The closest thing to human time might be decay. Let's assume that the operating systems that would need to retrieve one of those files have evolved so much that the file is unreadable in its current state. Its version is no longer supported. The other has not. It is still readable.

The unreadable file has aged in an abstract sense. Over centuries, operating systems were updated countless times, until it could no longer be read. But even then, the file is lost more to format than to time. The irretrievability of the file also doesn't mean death. If worthwhile, a bit of reverse engineering can render it readable again.

It's similar for delay. Retrieval time is the closest thing to delay in digital experience, but it is not temporal in the human sense, it is computational. It governs when information becomes actionable, not when it exists. A file can sit in storage for decades without "aging", but retrieval speed dictates its usability.

A .tiff file from 1998 and an .heic from 2025 might contain the same visual data, but they are optimized very differently. The .tiff will be substantially larger due to earlier technological constraints, and load more slowly than the .heic. The newer .heic becomes its preferred replacement.

In that sense, it is "aged" not by time but by tech context: a format timestamp rather than a temporal timestamp.

Digital age is relative, not absolute.

What is "old" is not determined by when it was created, but by how well it fits into the current computational architecture. In digital systems, time becomes a dimension of access, not existence. Events are stored as objects. Histories are not remembered; they are reloaded. Nothing truly ages in digital time. Data is always now.

The human self remains bound to lived time. The proxy self exists across asynchronous, compressible, and non-expiring time. These selves are coordinated by the same person, but their temporal realities are incompatible.

In the proxy condition, we are chrono-dual beings. To feel whole, we'll need to manage our two internal clocks, even though we only physically experience one.

CHAPTER SIXTEEN
Interior Integration

NOMOPHOBIA

My mug was warm in my hands.

My phone was face-down, but the screen stayed lit.

I didn't look at it. Not yet. This was new for me.

I sat still for a minute, but then flipped it over. Messages. A reminder for a meeting I was already dressed and ready for. I responded to my sister. Ignored Instagram. Deleted the alert.

My smartwatch was reminding me to get up and walk. No time.

I shoved my phone into the side pocket of my backpack. I meant to leave it there.

I didn't.

I don't remember taking it out of my backpack. The next thing I knew, I was in the meeting room waiting for the group, scrolling.

We do check our notifications. We will continue to. Most people live in both a physical and digital reality, all day, every day.

Fortunately, we do have the capacity to adapt to this duality. If we recognize it, name it, we can consciously develop it into infusus.

> **Infusus**
> noun
> /in-ˈfyù-səs/
>
> A state of sustained coherence across digital and physical systems, in which a person's values, agency, and presence remain continuous despite being filtered through incompatible frames of recognition.

A portion of the population already has, without knowing it.

TWO INTENTIONAL SELVES

During my research phase for this book, I conducted an interview with an eighteen-year-old, demographic: male, Black, suburban, upper-middle class, a senior in high school.

At night, he told me, he is an avid gamer. He has been friends with basically the same group of gamers for a few years. They know one another well, never having met in person. When I asked him about their interactions, he laughed.

"Profanity-laced, but friendly and intellectual," he said.

I asked him about school. He said his grades were "fine," and his attendance was "very good." His family moved before high school. He's still friends with the old friend group in the other town. They hang out every weekend, call and text throughout the week. He doesn't talk to anyone at the new school. He doesn't want to. He says he has enough friends.

Here's where it got interesting. I asked if he used profanity in everyday life. His appearance was clean-cut and conservative. His hair was neat, in symmetrical twists, not too long and not too short. Up to that point, he had been articulate and respectful. No swearing.

"No, I never really swear, except once in a great while when I'm driving by myself and someone cuts me off," he told me. This was believable.

I asked him if he had an avatar. He looked at me like I had asked him if he had a foot. So, I continued, "Would you wear that avatar on a t-shirt?"

"No," he replied, "it's something that looks good on the screen, but I wouldn't wear it to school or anything like that."

I pointed out that his physical and online presence were different. After considering that for a moment, he agreed. To most people born in the digital age, duality is a given.

As our conversation continued, it became clear to me that he is completely comfortable with both versions of himself. He did not view that as a split or a problem. Both were intentional. He understood they were context-specific, even if he didn't quite know what words to use.

His online persona was shaped by the norms of his digital environment, just as his offline behavior reflected the expectations of school and family.

Psychologists have long studied role-based behavior and code-switching, but often fail to recognize digital expression as part of that continuum. This high-school student had already integrated both. What theorists still struggle with, this guy had already resolved through practice.

After the interview, he asked me what my project was. I told him I was writing this book. For another twenty minutes, he asked astute questions.

Finally, he said, "I don't know of a scientist or expert that gets this wrong. I just think they're missing pieces."

Studies show that the kind of compartmentalization that comes naturally to this young man isn't inherently destabilizing. It only becomes harmful when the roles someone holds feel incompatible or morally at odds. Researchers have found that people can manage different roles in their lives, like being a parent, a friend, and a professional, without losing their sense of self, as long as those roles feel connected in a meaningful way.

Others have shown that switching between roles throughout the day is common and healthy, as long as the values behind those roles are consistent. In other words, integrity doesn't require you to act the same in every context. What matters is having a clear sense of how those roles fit together.

When the digital and physical self are both understood and shaped by the same internal compass, holding both can feel coherent, not conflicting.

AUTONOMY

Our reactions, behaviors, and decisions are not hard-coded. We do have autonomy, not only over ourselves, but collectively over the digital realm as a whole.

But the digital world is much larger than our brains or our bodies, so autonomy will probably never look linear.

First, let's dispel some common notions. Autonomy exists as self-governance, which is a neutral state. The individual or system determines its own course. In an ideal environment, it does so free from influence or manipulation. Decisions should originate from internal reasoning or values.

Yet, the word "autonomy" is commonly misused as a justification for impulsive behavior, rather than understood as a structured, long-range capacity for self-governance.

That's the paradox. Autonomy is not just freedom from others. It is also freedom from compulsion, impulse, and unexamined reaction. True autonomy often involves self-imposed structure: boundaries, commitments, and sustained effort aligned with one's chosen direction. Sometimes, it doesn't even feel like freedom.

A person may wake up tired, one weekday morning, and rationalize that they have a right to sleep in if they want to. That's true. Yet, if they were relying on their true autonomy, the preferred choice would be to keep their job. The person sleeping in may feel autonomous, but if they're risking their job or sabotaging their goals, they're ceding long-term authorship for short-term comfort.

In a world of infinite prompts and instant permission, the shape of autonomy must be redrawn. We need to see it less as a one-off reaction, more as internal authorship, resistant to drift.

As philosopher Byung-Chul Han writes, *"The subject of performance voluntarily exploits itself, believing itself to be free."*

In the digital sphere, autonomy is easily mistaken for freedom of choice, when in fact it often plays out as participation in structures we did not choose.

COGNITIVE EVOLUTION

The proxy condition isn't just a side effect of too many screens, nor merely an app, a space, or a habit. It is a living architecture. One that overlays presence, identity, and time. It asks us to exist in two dimensions at once. One physical. One digital. And while those dimensions often blur, their demands are different. The body seeks rest. The timeline refreshes. The self fragments. Within this structure, coherence is no longer a given. It must be designed.

The way I envision it, **cognitive evolution now looks like this**.

Fig. 16:1 The Five Domains of Today's Cognitive Coherence
A visual framework illustrating the key components of internal clarity in the dual self.

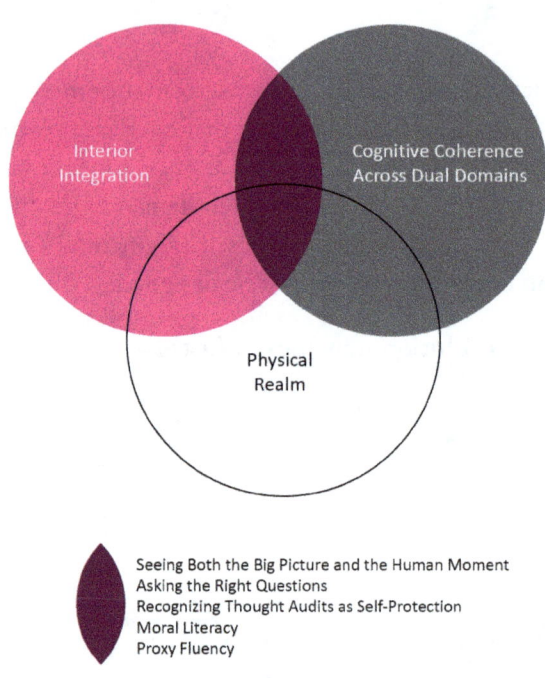

COGNITIVE COHERENCE ACROSS THE PROXY LINE

In this figure, we see our physical selves merging with cognitive coherence and interior integration. At the bottom, five components (or domains) are listed. All are uniquely human. AI can simulate aspects of them all, but fundamentally lacks the ability to weight, or feel them properly. Here's why AI will never replicate these well:

Seeing Both the Big Picture and the Human Moment

AI can scale data, but it cannot scale empathy. Humans can intuitively bridge macro patterns and individual nuance. We can 'just feel it' when context matters more than principle. Think of the countless meanings of "bless your heart" to a Southerner.

 AI can't sense when a systemic issue shows up in a single interaction. The ability to hold multiple layers of meaning at once, intuitively and emotionally, not just logically, is uniquely human. If you ask AI to give an overview, it will actually give you a one-dimensional analysis. That's all it has to offer.

Questions That Are Insightful

AI can generate questions, but not purposeful curiosity. Real insight depends on knowing what's missing, what's being avoided, or what's been too easily accepted. The right question often appears irrational or unprovable until hindsight reveals its power. AI can only model probability, not disruption with intent.

Recognizing Thought Audits as Self-Protection

AI cannot be threatened, so it cannot self-intervene. Humans protect their logic by noticing when they're being manipulated by others, by media, by themselves. This pattern recognition arises from vulnerability and lived memory. AI doesn't self-protect because it doesn't have a self.

Moral Literacy

AI can simulate ethics, but not moral weight. It also has no stake in being right or good. It lacks accountability. Moral literacy is learned through these things.

Proxy Fluency

AI is the proxy; it cannot outsmart itself. To be fluent in the proxy condition is to know when you're not being yourself. Humans know when they're being manipulated, influenced, or misrepresented. That ability to know requires reflective detachment from a role you're currently playing. AI has no detachment, only execution.

Our role in this dual existence begins to take shape and have real meaning. The goal is not collapse, but *infusus*, alignment without erasure.

Your relational clarity is like your Superman suit. It's the most powerful internal compass you have in today's world.

INTERIOR INTEGRATION

Leading psychoanalysts describe integration is the process of becoming psychologically whole. The idea is that different parts of the self, including unconscious impulses and conflicting motivations, are brought into alignment.

Infusus involves that process, and the integration of one more piece, our digital presence. What we're after is the alignment of perception, and intention across both selves.

RE-SETTING OURSELVES APART

I can already hear some of you thinking, *"I haven't even managed to do the first part yet."*

I'd like to point out that total mastery of any of these is impossible for both human and machine. We don't need to have all the answers. I definitely don't, and even if I did for a split second, the so-called "answers" would quickly change. It's not about being the smartest person in the room, or the most evolved. It's about being a human being. You're good at that.

We all carry assumptions. When people speak, we relate with our own stories. And, yeah, we make snap judgments. And we tend to keep falling back on all of these because, at some point, they worked for us. That's normal and healthy. The invitation here isn't to tear anything down. It's simply to pause long enough to ask, "Where did this come from?", "Is this still true for me?", or the most important of all, "Is this true in this particular context?"

There's a tendency, especially in talk therapy spaces, to treat self-reflection like a spotlight moment. As if every insight should be profound. As if every pause should produce transformation. But not all self-awareness has to be cinematic, with dramatic music swelling in the background. Understanding where we pick up after data leaves off automatically makes the picture much clearer.

In the case of the digital world around you, and your dual selves, a baseline awareness is really all you need. Just enough to not unconsciously allow the system to re-draw who you are.

FROM PARTICIPANT TO ARCHITECT

I worked for a company for a while where I was in charge of the IT department. At that particular company, the C-suite as they call it, was small. There were few executives. For lack of a better place to put me, they had me reporting to the CFO. The arrangement worked out fine, she was cool. She used to say to me, "I wish I knew all you did about computers."

The truth is, I wish I knew half of what she did about finance.

If there is a moral to that story, it is that we all have our areas of expertise, even if yours is just that you care.

Most people will never be coders. They do not care to create Python scripts or write a cloud-native application in Golang. During the early days, you'd need to have some skills like these, if you wanted to be a digital creator.

That's not the case anymore. It hasn't been for a while. WordPress, SquareSpace, and numerous others, allow everyday users to create backend functionality I used to code from scratch. Lately, AI does a lot of everyone's coding for them anyway, regardless of the language. Copy + paste and you're done. Nowadays, you don't need to be a developer to be a creator.

To take that a step further, you don't even need to work in tech, or have a job at all. Your mere presence makes you an architect. Presence is participation. Participation is authorship now.

Our goal? Simply to understand our role as system architects, and remember that we have instincts that artificial intelligence lacks. We also have the agency to re-draw the map, and keep re-drawing it whenever we want to.

Fig. 16:2 Modes of Presence and Perception

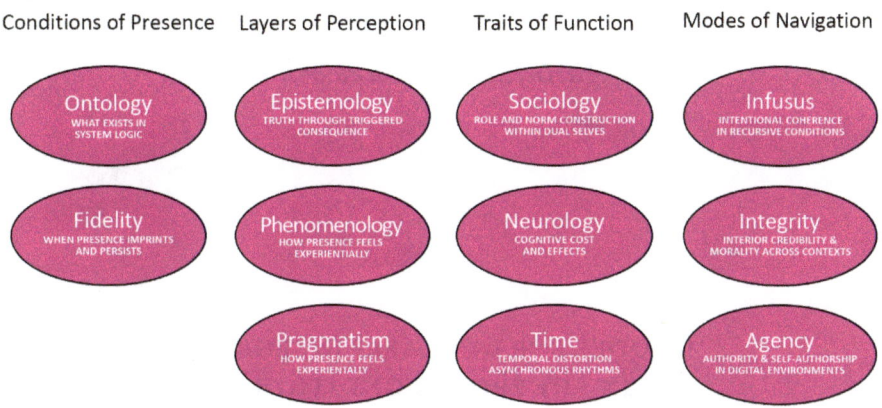

In the digital realm, identity begins with impact. What matters is what acts. What's real is what changes the system.

Presence, agency, and persistence are system thresholds. Cross over those and you leave a mark, you shape the system, whether you mean to or not.

That's the essence of the proxy state.

CHAPTER SEVENTEEN

An Infusus Framework

A MODEL FOR DUAL-SELF INTEGRITY IN THE PROXY CONDITION

"It was the best of times, it was the worst of times" is the opening line of Charles Dickens' *A Tale of Two Cities*. He could imagine two cities.

What he could not imagine was what it means to live in two worlds.

Dickens' reaction would have probably been wonder, not skepticism. He might have marveled at the possibilities.

Despite the tension, these may still be "the best of times". Living in two worlds offers a double horizon. It allows for reinvention. It gives space to those whose first self was defined for them. The second self is rewarding, more often than not, and rarely a trap.

Sometimes it is a platform, where people find a voice, where they test new truths, or where they finally feel seen.

Our virtual existence offers a nonjudgmental space for autonomy, experimentation, and identity. Visibility and opportunity have been democratized, and that's a very good thing. Influence is no longer gatekept by institutions, corporations, or agents. A compelling idea or creative act can reach a global audience, regardless of credentials, pedigree, or zip code. It gives voice even to those on the margins of society.

Time zones no longer limit presence. The online community can offer support, share insight, and express love or solidarity without needing to be in the same place, or even awake at the same time. Lifelong friendships are not torn apart the way they once were, simply because one person moved away. People with disabilities can be whole. Those who live in rural areas can feel close by, and connected.

At its best, the digital self creates a living record, a journal of thoughts, moments, and growth. It can help us remember those we've lost, not only through photographs but by preserving small details that once defined their presence.

On any given day, we are living, and we are also broadcasting, constructing, presenting, responding, and being read. The duality is no longer emerging. It has arrived. And we are already inside it, fully integrated.

Let's briefly revisit my chat with Uncle Henley, the one who said, "I don't use a computer."

I'll just reiterate here that online presence is inescapable. Your location can be tracked by security cameras, at traffic lights and toll booths, your purchases logged through loyalty cards, and your prescriptions stored in cloud-based records. Your movements, and even your DNA, can be inferred through someone else. As mentioned, even silence is measured.

That's particularly notable because it qualifies Odell's choice of rejecting digital life or embracing it. We do have the option to put our phones down more often, and we should. But realistically, the choice has already been made for us.

It's not inherently a bad one if we look clearly at what we've built, and consider what it might allow us to become, if carried with intention.

Here's the good news: shaping this into a mindful, rewarding existence is far easier to accomplish than one might think. We already live in duality. Our perspective just needs to catch up.

Fig. 17:1 Unevolved Identity Structures
Fragmented identity in the digital era.

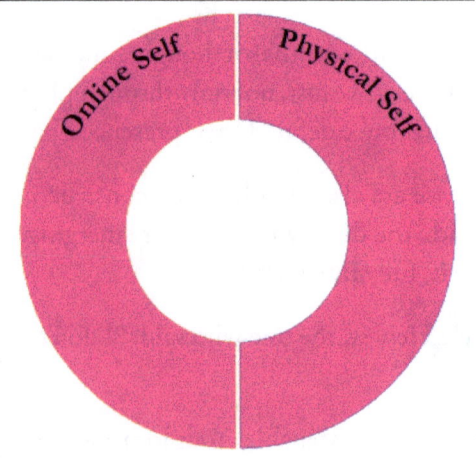

By default, our two identity structures sit side by side. In that state, they can hold unaligned value systems. The result is the felt conflict we've been describing.

We have an unfortunate human instinct that compels us to *name* anything we perceive to be "wrong" with us, so this state is often mistaken for inattentiveness, fatigue, a lack of sense of belonging, irritability, or disassociation.

Fig. 17:2 Evolving Identity Structures
Integrating dual identities in the digital era.

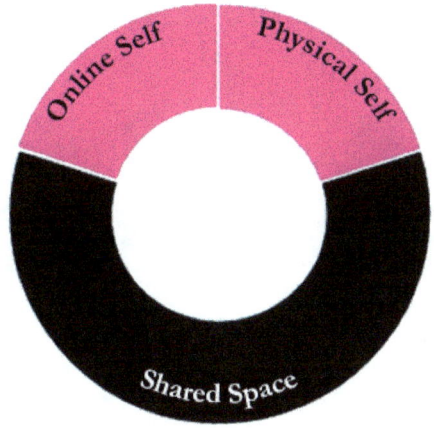

In our quest to feel whole, our next level of recognition as a society, is for every individual to recognize their own commonalities between their two selves and create a shared space.

Some scholars have urged integration at this point. The shared space should have quite a bit of commonality, the parts of you that are the same in both the digital and physical states. But there are many aspects of both that can't be integrated.

Instead, once a coherent identity is identified, grounded in both awareness and alignment, it will be used to guide both our physical and digital selves. This figure shows the two selves nested above a grounded, shared space I'll call *infusus*. The parts are now aligned intentionally, working together, but not quite yet as a whole. They are still divided segments of one psyche.

The proxy condition is agnostic to our well-being. What determines its impact on us personally is whether we achieve infusus, a structural coherence between selves, or lose ourselves due to saturation and interference.

Fig. 17:3 Infusus
Integrated identity in the digital era.

Logically, if we look for that coherence, a way to connect the parts, the next step would be to integrate into that shared space between the digital and physical selves.

This can easily be misinterpreted. If the two could simply be joined, duality wouldn't exist. It's too simplistic to assume we can just meld them together. The premise doesn't hold; the logic fails.

You could look at it another way; if that were possible, then our physical and digital selves would have to, by design, be the same. They are not of course. Nor do we want them to be.

Infusus is not to be confused with fusion. Instead, we're trying to piece together the parts in a way that they do *not* blend, but coexist.

So instead of fusion, we need two separate realms that are **mutually consequential**.

Ideally, infusus refuses the loss of either self, and can accept a certain amount of contradiction. We're not trying to collapse the digital and the physical into a single presence. We can allow ourselves to be both without allowing either to dominate.

The digital and the physical aren't two halves of one self. They're two presences, held in tension through shared authorship.

At its most basic level, infusus is acceptance. It's a steady alignment where the two versions of self no longer play tug-of-war with your focus. They inform each other without distraction, because we've come to accept the tension and understand it's not a flaw. It's the meeting point of two distinct forms of your autonomy, both working within you.

Infusus is adaptive autonomy.

AUTONOMY IN DUALITY

In an earlier section, we talked about autonomy. Let's reexamine it through the lens of infusus.

If there are two distinct forms inside us, with a shared space between, it makes sense that some of our value system is unique to each. During the interview with the high school student, he admitted he swears profusely when he games, but his physical self hardly ever does. He doesn't experience it as hypocrisy. He sees it as context-aware behavior.

This divided state is unprecedented, but we can draw somewhat of a parallel to Jonathan Haidt's Moral Foundations Theory (MFT).

Haidt separates our morality into six categories: Care, which centers on empathy and the protection of others from harm, Fairness, which focuses on justice, reciprocity, and equality, Loyalty, which values allegiance to one's group or community, Authority, which emphasizes respect for tradition, leadership, and social order, Sanctity, which relates to purity, both physical and moral, and the avoidance of degradation, and Liberty, which concerns the resistance to domination and the defense of personal freedom.

With infusus, the shared space will share many, if not most, of what we consider morally non-negotiable. What we personally view as right or wrong, and what we prioritize, both our physical self and our digital self will share.

Haidt then goes on to say that a functioning society needs to recognize and balance multiple moral foundations, even if some seem foreign or uncomfortable.

Infusus adds another level of understanding to that balance. It expands to include those instances where the two sides don't share the same belief.

In the example of the high school student, that would look like this:

Fig. 17:4 Stratified Morality
The high school student in our example has two systems drawing from the same core principles but applying them differently.

The shared space holds what both selves consider non-negotiable.

The divided space reflects how each self adapts to its environment. The digital self may embrace liberty and fairness more strongly, while the physical self clings more to sanctity or authority. Up to now, the consensus has been that these shifts as betrayals. Infusus reidentifies them as adaptations. They're evidence of something that has been there since we crossed the proxy line, an expanded moral code that is responsive, not uniform.

To some, it may seem that freedom of choice has collapsed under systemic pressure, and that's why the teenager in our example uses so much profanity when he games. The premise is, gaming is eroding our morality. "Kids these days" have less of a moral framework than the pre-digital generations had.

But the fact that the teenager can detect that stratification, that he can trace it, name it, and question it, is evidence of something still intact.

We do have quite a bit of micro-agency left within our digital world. For the most part, we choose the apps, the platforms, and everything within them. There are still opportunities for us opt out, or perform tasks manually and circumvent the internet altogether, but that's not where our autonomy is really leveraged, since silence is also measured. We reclaim agency not by escaping the proxy, but by editing it. By making sure the choices we make aren't the ones being presented to us, but rather the ones we choose.

This is control we possess. Infusus is agency because it preserves volition where full control is no longer possible.

That agency has the potential to allow us to shape the future. However, I don't envision us reclaiming full control in the traditional sense. Not when we're dealing with a once-in-humanity, multi-faceted phenomenon.

Instead, we can avoid inadvertently relinquishing the autonomy we have to entities seeking to profit from it. Adopting infusus means we recognize the influence and reassert authorship from within.

In doing so, we author a dual presence that is adaptive. One that can shape the systems it occupies, without losing itself inside them.

PART III

THE COGNITIVE HOME SCREEN

CHAPTER EIGHTEEN

The Ethics of Attention

"The greatest threat to deep thinking today isn't ignorance. It's interruption."

- Cal Newport, author of Deep Work

YOUR FOCUS IS THE PRODUCT

You didn't write the article. You just clicked. But so did a million others. Together, you made it go viral.

What shows up next, for you and for everyone else, is shaped by that small, ordinary moment. The system doesn't know why you clicked, or didn't. It doesn't need to. It just assumes you'll do it again.

So, if our attention is the product, what does it look like for content creators, big business, social media outlets and AI to maintain an ethical presence?

THE REALITY

Ad-based revenue models (Google, Meta, TikTok) depend on maximum scroll time and emotional intensity. Outrage performs. Novelty performs.

Content creators often have to chase algorithmic visibility. That means using urgency, trend exploitation, and sometimes manipulative hooks just to stay visible.

Big tech's feedback loops are built on user telemetry: what we click, abandon, linger on. This behavioral data is the raw fuel for refinement and monetization.

AI tools, even at their most helpful, risk being optimized toward retention, not value. Retention feeds training data. Usage metrics guide funding.

SO WHAT'S POSSIBLE WITHIN THE SYSTEM?

For content providers, survival demands some attention capture. That isn't any different than a street with a string of car dealerships on it, all competing to draw you in. That doesn't mean we can't do better. Creating a culture where customer demand includes responsible content creation is important.

Big tech does not operate on a moral framework. Decisions are based on reach, efficiency, and return. Some harm is tolerable as long as it does not disrupt growth. That's why it seems like Mark Zuckerberg is always testifying before congress. This doesn't mean his, or any other companies are malicious. It means they are structured to optimize systems, not ethics.

Ethical design *is* possible. Most platforms could be built to protect attention, limit friction, and prioritize user autonomy. But in a capitalist society, altruism often isn't the goal. Their entire business model depends on maximizing your time, data, and money. Their choice is deliberate, and baked into their code.

In all likelihood, ethical design will not be prioritized unless pressure is exerted from the outside: regulation that sets boundaries, public scrutiny that affects reputation, or cultural movements that redefine acceptable practice. Until incentives change, design will often reflect what platforms can get away with, not what users actually need.

Influencers and creators face a different set of pressures. Their income depends on remaining visible within systems designed to reward spectacle, repetition, and polarization. Since platforms measure success in engagement, not integrity, creators often face a tradeoff between reach and restraint. Many care deeply about their audience, but the platform logic pushes them to prioritize content that performs over content that reflects.

In addition, if you take a quick look at a few short clips from influencers, you'll almost immediately recognize that anyone with a camera and charisma can broadcast ideas to millions. Simple ignorance plays a bigger role than we admit. There's no vetting process. There is no way of knowing if a teenage beauty influencer has tested her methods for safety, or on different types of skin, or if the guy on YouTube telling you how to fix your freezer didn't break his own ice machine twice while trying. We can't assume these people know what they're doing.

On the other hand, there those who do know better, and purposely skew content. If I were to read that sentence out loud in a room, and ask the group what first came to mind upon hearing those words, there would be very few who didn't say X, or Twitter. And while Elon Musk might be one of the more public examples, he definitely isn't the only one guilty of pushing dangerous propaganda.

In a free-speech, democratic environment, citizens like you and me have chosen that to be their right. We, as a society, have a responsibility.

As we create a dialogue around intentionally developing a proxy self that accurately represents us, exercising free speech responsibly should be a top priority. Here are some things for your proxy self to consider:

Respecting Diverse Viewpoints

Democracy thrives on pluralism. Individuals must be willing to hear and tolerate views they may strongly disagree with, as long as those views don't incite violence or harm.

This doesn't mean endorsing every opinion, but defending the right of others to express them.

Engaging Thoughtfully and Honestly

It's surprising how many people mistakenly interpret "free speech" as the ability to say whatever you want. According to our constitution, "Congress shall make no law... abridging the freedom of speech, or of the press..."

Still, in our country's history, the court system has repeatedly held that a lot of the discourse you and I hear every day is less protected, or even unprotected speech. Incitement to imminent violence, true threats, obscenity, defamation, libel, slander, speech integral to criminal conduct and certain forms of commercial speech (like false advertising).

The reason that is true is simple. We don't push back. A healthy democracy requires a well-informed public. Citizens have a responsibility to demand accurate reporting, resist propaganda, and support independent journalism. Now, more than ever, it's crucial that the public strives to hold companies, individuals and institutions accountable.

Protecting Free Speech for All, Not Just Some

It's easy to support free speech when it's your own. The real test of democratic commitment is defending the rights of others. Especially unpopular minorities or dissenting voices.

Distinguishing Between Free Speech and Consequences

People must understand that while free speech protects you from government censorship, it does not shield you, or anyone else, from social consequences. You have the right to respond, debate, or reject ideas you find harmful or false. Others have the right to respond to you the same way.

ATTENTION BECOMES SYSTEMIC ARCHITECTURE

Before the digital age, the average person reserved the bandwidth they had to focus on their home, their work, their family, and a few major world events. Now, we absorb the grief of strangers, the outrage of headlines, the curated envy of digital perfection - all before breakfast.

We're told that attention shapes belief. But belief isn't being shaped by depth. It's being shaped by interruption. The digital world doesn't ask for discernment. It asks for reaction. It interrupts what clarity you were building, and then offers up cognitive clutter in its place.

That would be troubling enough. But what makes it systemic is what happens next.

UNCHOSEN INFRASTRUCTURE SHAPES BELIEF

No hyperbole here; this is nothing short of dangerous if not understood.

We assume we choose our feed. But what's left out becomes more influential than what's included.

Censorship comes to mind first. Little needs to be said about that. The suppression of content for political purposes has always been an issue and continues to be. Extending this theory beyond simple censorship, we also experience quiet exclusion of everyday, harmless content through deliberate design. The algorithm is an invisible force, guiding you in a prescribed direction, all under the illusion that you're choosing it.

You can't notice what you never saw. We exist in an attention economy that favors urgency over value, and that is a breeding ground for misinformation.

The invisible algorithm. A filter that shapes which issues feel urgent, which stories repeat, and what people accept as normal. We, as a society, need to pause and think about this, because it doesn't just affect individuals. It affects policy. It affects precedent. It informs how court cases are interpreted, what gets covered in hearings, and which public figures are considered credible.

In other words, we may want to believe that the algorithm is just reflecting preference. It's really good at convincing us; "your feed" "for you", "your timeline."

In reality, behind the scenes it is manufacturing consensus. It builds familiarity, then treats that familiarity as legitimacy.

We know that when misinformation is rewarded with engagement, it multiplies as a result. So, if your attention drifts toward mockery, outrage, or aesthetic without substance, those things will naturally become more prominent, extending beyond your feed and into our collective consciousness. The algorithm is paying attention, yes. But so are you. And you're a paycheck to someone.

As a society, nobody warned us to do what we already know. Fact-check. Don't repost hoaxes. Ignore sensationalized content. Click responsibly. This isn't about discipline. It's about calibration. It's the difference between what catches your eye and what truly earns your attention.

Your private self probably feels immune. I know mine stubbornly (and falsely) does. But what we consume quietly shapes what we speak aloud.

The reality is, sometimes, who we give our attention to is the only real power we have left.

ATTENTION COERCION

Attention isn't neutral. Before any deliberate action occurs, it has our attention. It is often just a split second between us noticing something, and reacting to it. We notice a headline, we tap it.

This is critical because it reframes attention not as a personal failing or lifestyle habit, but as an entry point. If someone controls your attention, they're deciding what even shows up for your conscience to consider.

Attention coercion is the deliberate design of digital interfaces that guide users toward maximum engagement, intentionally overriding their original intent.

Users are not powerless, but they are often miscast as passive participants in systems they actually help sustain.

Engagement becomes powerful when it is metacognitive.

Power in digital environments does not lie in avoiding them. It lies in understanding how your participation shapes the very systems you move through.

SOLUTIONISM

Author Evgeny Morozov has long argued that what he calls "solutionism" in tech culture masks complexity with convenience. In his view, systems that promise solutions (or answers) often do so by shrinking the scope of acceptable questions.

He argues that tech companies often claim to have "answers," but in doing so, they narrow the problem. Instead of dealing with the full messy reality, they redefine the problem into something their tool can fix.

For example, instead of asking "Why are people unhealthy?", a fitness app might just ask "How many steps did you take today?"

It feels like a solution, but it hides deeper issues. Like access to healthcare, food quality, or working conditions. Suddenly, you're searching your phone for the fitness app you haven't looked at in months.

The digital realm is full of promises to make life easier. At times, in doing so, it can ignore what really needs to be asked.

That's Morozov's point. The "answer" is only as good as the question it allows, and those questions are often limited by the system offering the fix.

His concept met with controversy because it's iconoclastic. It questioned the ideological underpinnings of contemporary tech development and governance. Whether readers saw it as a vital critique or a hindrance to innovation depended on their assumptions about which problems tech should solve, and how tech should solve them.

I'm not here to settle that debate. But the question itself definitely belongs here, although not quite how Morozov originally framed it.

In 2013, when Morozov wrote those words, he used terms like "Silicon Valley" to describe the people responsible for solutionism.

He singled out content creators, a certain former Google CEO, and others in the field, all of whom were proponents of bigger web presence at that time. Back then, right or wrong, that was the right group for him to target.

Today, it means everyone.

Do I use AI to write my paper? Do I trust the search results' recommendations when I shop, or do I take the time to search for what I actually need? Does my cousin in Arizona rise to the level of a phone call or a personal visit, or am I okay with just keeping in touch on Facebook?

Jeff Jarvis, a long-time advocate of digital transparency, once argued that "publicness" would empower individuals by making them visible and heard. But what happens when visibility isn't voluntary, and being seen becomes a precondition of access?

Ironically, Jarvis was one of the people Morozov called out.

A LOOK AT MORALITY

If we're honest, morality was already changing in our times. But now, something deeper has shifted. The conversation has transcended what's right and wrong. We're starting to reconsider what morality even is. I debated whether I should include a section on morality in this book. It does somewhat contrast with the concept of digital duality being an external force. If that's true, then what does our morality have to do with it?

The answer is, our morality is so deeply linked to our sense of trust. In order to be discerning, we're all going to need to rethink moral literacy.

What does that look like in an age where we're acting, perceiving, and interpreting across two selves? Where there may be a shared baseline, or not?

A large group of people would like to unwind recent social progress. They believe that nontraditional gender identities, same-sex relationships, and immigrants who don't speak English are threats to the culture.

Another group sees that belief itself as immoral, inhumane, and rewinding progress.

The divide isn't just political. It's personal, philosophical, and emotional. It's getting harder to find common ground. And now, with dual presence layered on top, morality is even less of a fixed code. It also keeps shifting, depending on who is speaking and who is listening, depending on which channel you watch. Any individual can have many distinctly different moral codes at once. It's like walking through a hall of mirrors where each reflection insists it's the original.

Some types of righteousness can be crowd-sourced now. Someone posts a clip, a quote, a photo out of context. Suddenly, the internet decides who's good and who's not. The judgment feels fast, sharp, permanent. Until it isn't. Someone gets applauded one day, then scrutinized the next. Maybe even both at the same time.

Someone breaks a rule and is celebrated for being bold. Others cringe. The rules shift depending on who's watching and how it's framed. A singular moment can change the meaning of everything.

A lot of this has always been the case with morality. It was never black and white. Typically, unevenly applied. Usually, it was good to follow the rules, sometimes not.

The difference is the constant shift. What feels right in one moment may not hold in the next. A joke at a party was taken in context. Now it lives forever.

The internet's wide reach changed things. Doxxing, impersonation, fake reviews, widespread non-consensual sharing of an image of you or someone you love. The digital age has created new moral violations.

It's up to us to adapt, better understand, and be ready to look head-on at this new reality. Our collective misinterpretation of the digital age's effect on society came with a naivete that we'll need to rethink.

How does this translate to your dual self?

In The Righteous Mind, Jonathan Haidt wrote, "people don't adopt their ideologies at random, or by soaking up whatever ideas are around them."

He was describing a time when political identity could still be mapped along two lines that could both be framed as a version of morality. I say this as a fan of Haidt's work. His insights still hold. But the shape of choice has changed. That book was published in 2012, when our cognitive input still looked very different.

We are still predisposed. Haidt was right about that. But there is no rigidity anymore. We can't afford to resign ourselves to a "that's just the way I am" mindset. If we do, we tread into the area where the internet can be dangerous.

We can recognize that our digital moral choices are no longer made through slow moral intuitions over time, but through fast moral reactions over networks. This makes moral formation itself unstable, volatile, and reversible.

We should absolutely keep what we value, but we can realign. Just as humankind will continue to evolve along those same lines in the physical world, we can adjust our moral framework to work in a fluid, ever-changing environment.

It seems like we do a lot of talking about the problem: "A young girl was cyberbullied.", "Grandma fell for an internet scam."

The advice we get? "Be more careful." Not exactly helpful.

Instead, we need to expand our view of morality beyond simple, binary judgment to a layered view.

No matter what you lean toward in your physical state, your digital state may mirror that, to a degree. Yet, you carry both the self you shaped and the one that was shaped for you. As it relates to morality, we only need to expand our views to be less absolute.

In the digital age, morality isn't just what we believe, it's how fast we decide, how publicly we declare, and how long the echo lasts. The ethical question isn't only "what is right?" but "in which context, under whose gaze, and for how long?"

THE ECHO CHAMBER

I'll admit it. My personalized news feed is curated to my tastes. To me, it's calm, seems relatively balanced, and is often centered around topics I like to read about. I like it. It feels reasonable. Easy to scroll through to catch up on the topics of the day.

Just a tap away is the "Headlines" tab.

Same platform. Same day. But the tone shifts dramatically. Different language. Different focus. Entirely different emotional posture. If I always read that tab, I'd believe we were on the brink of civil collapse. If I always read mine, I might think everyone was working toward some kind of solution.

That's a distinct difference between broadcast television back in the day, and the curated, made-just-for-you content of today. And who, exactly, is making the decision what I see?

It's disorienting. In a sense, we're living in whichever chamber the interface decided to show us. The illusion of consensus sets in because all our sources agree with us.

The term "echo chamber" is a colloquialism that has been around for a long time. It means an environment where a person is primarily exposed to opinions, narratives, and information that reflect and reinforce their existing beliefs, while opposing viewpoints are minimized, dismissed, or entirely absent.

Ironically, that's almost identical to the definition of extremism.

It's easy to mock echo chambers as ideological traps. But they're not built out of beliefs. They're built out of habit. Nobody who is ever in one recognizes they are, until they're out. And the longer we stay inside them, the more extreme the outside starts to look.

We're not extremists. Yet.

CHAPTER NINETEEN
Temporal Jet Lag

IT'S NOT YOUR TIMELINE THAT'S OUT OF SYNC

You wake up and check your phone. A quick scroll becomes twelve minutes. You were in bed, but also inside six news cycles, a celebrity breakup, three global tragedies, two product launches, and the curated morning routines of people you don't know. All before your feet hit the ground.

And that's the moment the lag begins.

You leap out of bed, your lateness in physical time throwing you into a momentary panic.

Travel-induced jet lag happens when your body, specifically your circadian rhythm, moves faster than your internal clock can adjust. *Temporal* jet lag is when your attention does. Your digital self accelerates while your physical self stays. Two versions of you, operating in different temporal zones, on the same day.

The physiological underpinnings of physical and digital jet lag differ, but their effects are either the same, or very similar.

The symptoms can be subtle, or strong. Physically, this would likely reflect how many time zones you crossed along the way. Digitally, it would depend on what you missed, how long you were away, and the level of your own personal involvement (which may be the most analogous to the length of the trip).

Reentry into digital environments after a period of absence can result in an immediate spike in cognitive demand, often referred to as alert fatigue. Like physical jet lag, it impairs working memory and decision-making even in the absence of urgency.

You're disconnected from the hour you're in. You glance up from a screen and can't remember what you were doing before. The light in the room seems wrong. You're late to something, but it's not on your calendar. It's the sensation of being out of sync with your own day.

And it builds. You try to ground yourself by doing something productive, but your mind won't settle. You reach for your phone, seeking more input to regulate the overwhelm, which only makes the split worse. You're not over-scheduled. You're over-located. Mentally distributed across dozens of timelines, but not fully present in any of them.

The worst part? It feels personal. As if the fragmentation is a character flaw. As if everyone else has figured out how to manage their time, just not you. But this isn't a time management issue. It's time distortion.

We were not designed to shift mental contexts hundreds of times per day. The human brain didn't evolve to toggle between emotional registers so fast. To witness grief, irony, violence, sales tactics, and a childhood friend's vacation in a three-minute scroll.

Philosopher Byung-Chul Han observed that the modern age suffers from a "*disappearance of the contemplative temporal order.*" In essence, he means that today's world leaves too little room for reflection. Our lives are broken into fast-moving fragments, with less time for depth or continuity. When every moment is short, scattered, and on display, the experience of real duration disappears.

Temporal Jet Lag
noun
/ˈtem-p(ə-)rəl ˈjet ˌlag/

A cognitive disorientation caused by asynchronous time perception between the physical and digital self. It arises when attention accelerates beyond physical context, creating temporal mismatch.

We have exponentially more input, and still just twenty-four hours in a day. We weren't meant to metabolize it all, let alone all at once.

And so we lag.

Sometimes it shows up as a mild yet persistent sense of low-key anxiety. Sometimes as brain fog. Sometimes as that strange, haunting feeling that you're running behind in a life you're already living. The only clue is a faint dissonance. A sense that you're off, but the offness doesn't immediately connect with physical time because it's only *partly* physical time.

You haven't been lazy or unfocused. You have been reacting to stimuli that isn't in the room with you, because it's not physical.

Physical jet lag occurs because your body's rhythm (Circadian) is not in sync with the time of day it is currently in. Your body reacts to sunlight and darkness, and releases chemicals in the brain, like melatonin, synchronizing you to that cycle. If that is disrupted, there is a mismatch between your internal clock and what we'll call outer time.

This is striking. It shows us that presence is not only spacial. It is also temporal compatibility with the environment around you. Like physical jet lag, temporal jet lag is dislocation from a governing rhythm that continues without you.

It's also perplexing. There have been studies attempting to explain this condition.

In 2017, Leonard Reinecke said, in *Computers in Human Behavior,* "Digital multitasking environments correlate with increased stress and reduced affective well-being, creating a state similar to chronic low-grade anxiety."

A study published in Discover Mental Health surveyed 351 employees across various sectors, revealing that cybersecurity fatigue significantly contributes to burnout, reduced productivity, and increased psychological strain.

Another study in Technological Forecasting and Social Change highlighted the rapid intensification of digital burnout during the COVID-19 pandemic, attributing it to overwhelming internet consumption as people turned to digital platforms for work, leisure, and social activities.

Hundreds of millions of indexed results globally, across blogs, forums, articles, scientific papers, videos, Reddit threads, and even memes. The evidence speaks for itself. Temporal disorientation and fatigue from digital life is very widespread, even if it isn't yet precisely named. Stronger empirical validation is needed. Comparatively, it is easy to find empirical and anecdotal evidence.

Fig. 19:1 Estimated Impact Felt by Digital Burnout
Using roughly synonymous queries, I gathered evidence of how widespread this phenomenon appears to be. Here are the results as of May, 2025.

QUERY TYPE	EXAMPLE TERMS	ESTIMATED RESULT VOLUME*
Digital fatigue / burnout	"digital fatigue," "Zoom fatigue," "screen burnout"	10M – 100M+
Tech-related sleep disruption	"screens affecting sleep," "blue light insomnia," "technology and circadian rhythms"	5M – 50M+
Information overload / cognitive fatigue	"alert fatigue," "too much information tired," "online cognitive overload"	1M – 20M
Always-on culture / digital exhaustion	"feeling tired from being online," "social media exhaustion," "can't unplug"	1M – 10M
Time distortion / dissociation	"lost track of time online," "digital time distortion," "scrolling dissociation"	500K – 5M

Comparatively, search results are extremely scarce for phrases that express the opposite, like "the internet gives me more energy," or "I sleep better if I surf more in bed."

In fact, there was an entire Reddit thread called /nosurf. It has since been deleted, but at the time of this writing was still up, searchable and readable. Its title was, *"Why does entertainment on internet make me tired?"*

Its subtitle read, *"When I load up youTube or any other entertainment after an hour I feel physically tired, when I wake up in the morning with no media and do something else I have more energy compared to when i use my phone or laptop"*

In the sub, there are several anecdotes that sum this up. One poster, with a since-deleted account said, *"Due to context switching. When you juggle around content your mind takes lots of energy to switch the context , which makes you feel tired."*

Another posted, *"when I load up youTube or any other entertainment after an hour I feel physically tired, when I wake up in the morning with no media and do something else I have more energy compared to when i use my phone or laptop."*

The posts appear above as originally written. Spelling and grammar have not been corrected.

This mismatch between presence and perception has crept quietly into our days. It fragments attention, disorients our internal compass, and leaves us depleted without explanation.

Our minds, shaped by evolutionary timelines, aren't designed to process so many shifts in context, tone, and consequence in such rapid succession. The result isn't just digital fatigue. It's something closer to cognitive disorientation, one that manifests physiologically, psychologically, and socially. Recent studies back this up. When we try to live on digital time, we fall out of sync with the biological and social cycles that once grounded us.

CHAPTER TWENTY
An Asynchronous Clock

THE HERE AND WHEN

If temporal jet lag is the feeling, the asynchronous digital clock is the source.

It's an invisible flow we've all been syncing to, without realizing. There are only a few. We call them flows, rhythms, cycles.

Physical time, of course, is the primary one. Let's make an important distinction here. The concept of time measurement is different than time itself.

There are Circadian rhythms, our body's internal "clock" that regulates when we sleep, wake, our temperature, digestion, and other physiological processes. They're known as zeitgebers Light is the most powerful one. We wake to the sunlight.

Interdisciplinary research lists many other temporal systems. We're limiting the scope to these three for a few reasons:

First, cultural ritual cycles (like holidays), institutional timelines (school, government), and even strong contenders like menstrual cycles, are encompassed by variants of these two.

Second, we'll exclude any others that require external reinforcement (e.g. social agreement, attention, observance). It's not a true temporal system if you have to opt in.

Last, we'll limit the scope to those that apply to human beings, since frogs don't have a TikTok.

Treating digital engagement as a kind of parallel time has some precedent in media studies, but here's where it becomes esoteric. In my research, I discovered that there is no single, canonical list of attributes used across disciplines (e.g., chronobiology, philosophy of time, cognitive science) to define a temporal system. That surprised me. I believe that's why the theory never went any further.

But there was enough overlap to construct a pattern. What follows is an original synthesis of that pattern: five operational criteria proposed here as the minimum bar for what qualifies as a governing time-state. These are not drawn from a single field, but derived from recurring themes across biological, philosophical, and behavioral frameworks.

Autonomous Operation

In order to qualify as a temporal state, it must continue to function and evolve without user participation or awareness. It cannot require attention, memory, or engagement.

The digital world moves forward in time constantly, with or without us.

Directional Progression

To meet these criteria, it needs to unfold in a structured, non-reversible sequence. It has an inherent ordering (e.g., day follows night, updates age, feeds decay) and cannot be reset arbitrarily.

On a digital platform, every piece of content is assigned a timestamp. From that moment forward, the system applies time-based logic to it. Things can move down in a feed, expire, re-sort or even archive. You go to pay your cable bill and the site has been redesigned. You may be able to scroll back to view it again, or re-engage, but you can't undo that fact that temporal aging has taken place.

Consequential Impact Without Engagement

The system exerts influence on you even when ignored. You close your laptop. You don't post. You don't scroll. You don't receive a single message. For 36 hours, you are completely disconnected.

During that time, your device (without your input) logs you out of websites, recalculates content queues, flushes cached conversations, archives data, and downgrades algorithmic importance for content you never saw. Deleted items set to permanently delete after 30 days have passed that time and are now gone.

The system evolves internally: files age, timestamps advance, feeds reorder based on temporal logic you did not witness. When you log back in, the system exists in a new present state, different than it would have if you had logged on a few hours before. You didn't miss anything. You simply missed the passing of something very much like time. Anything that you do differently now, or don't do, as a result, demonstrates that there is consequential impact.

Systemic Pressure to Re-align

A temporal state will create a physical desire within us to re-synchronize. This is similar to the zeitgebers of circadian rhythms.

In the digital realm, notifications, updates, and online interactions act as artificial zeitgebers, prompting us to adjust our behaviors and attention spans to the rhythm of digital platforms.

That's the jet lag. Your aunt calls to ask if you've seen pictures of the new baby. You haven't. You try to look for them while the two of you are still on the phone, but the post was from days ago. It's so far down your feed now, you can't easily find it.

You haven't opened your fitness app in several days. When you return, your goal streak is broken, the dashboard displays warnings, and your weekly average is flagged in red. You feel an immediate desire to walk.

You log back into a task management app and see a sea of overdue alerts. You weren't notified directly, but the pressure to "get back in sync" is immediate.

This illustrates that there now exists another system that governs human experience in the way only time systems do: persistently, directionally, autonomously, and consequentially.

The three have a functional equivalence, yet they're very different.

Earlier in the chapter, I mentioned that the concept of time measurement is different than time itself. This is how that plays out:

The asynchronous clock is the substrate. Social norms, platform manipulation, or attention loops occur on it like a timeline, just as other events occur on clocks and calendars. Asynchronous digital time is not defined by the volume of tasks, but rather, the system that underlies them doing its work. Tasks proliferate because the substrate invites constant re-engagement

Some might argue, "But that's just Instagram culture!"

But if you take a deeper look, the Instagram post was what the system *produced*. The digital clock is what made it possible, by being there: rhythmic and governing. By shaping us even when we're not consciously aware.

I'm also not claiming that asynchronous digital time is natural, only that it has come to function as time in the full phenomenological and behavioral sense.

Unlike in the physical dimension, the asynchronous clock is uneven in its pace. There is no hour or day. It begins each time you unlock your phone or receive a new notification. It's inviting you to catch up, stay current, and never quite stop. It ends when you move on to whatever is next; a new notification, clickbait, or something in the physical room that catches your attention.

In other words, our physical time moves forward at the same measured pace it always has, since the beginning of creation. Same with our body clock. Our hearts still beat in a rhythm, as they have since our own physical birth. Digital time loops, accelerates and slows down. As it does, we can feel our own unique pattern unfolding in time.

If it is out of sync. We feel a lag, and a pull to realign.

Fig. 20:1 Measuring Time in Two Dimensions
A comparison of how time is tracked and felt in physical versus digital contexts; one shared and steady, the other personal and variable.

LINEAR TIME	DIGITAL TIME
Measured by seconds/minutes	Measured by time spent connected
Moves at a constant rate	Varies (surges, stalls, resets)
Shared across people	Personalized & unique
Synchronized by physics	Asynchronous, driven by algorithms, interactions, and attention loops.

The digital part of this duality is the structure.

Writers like Cal Newport and James Williams have argued that regaining attention and intentionality requires redesigning the architecture of focus.

I wholeheartedly agree, but to make that goal attainable, we're going to have to reimagine the internal structure of presence itself so that we can live across systems without fragmenting who we are. I've referred to that as interior integrity.

Let's unpack the source of the dissonance: You are physically in your day, but you are also mentally in dozens of other people's. Sometimes you're inside their yesterday. You're operating in asynchronous time, but with a nervous system hard-wired for unchanging seconds, minutes, hours and days. Your heart beats in rhythm. The asynchrony occurs because, at the same time, there is a second, external, temporal force that ebbs and flows to an uneven beat.

You look up into the physical room and try to re-enter that reality, but the day moved on so you need to reorient. You glance at your messages and see five threads unfolding without you. You open your news feed and see three global tragedies already fully discussed. It feels like you're late, but not to anything specific. You're just late to now. Here's the thing; in both zones, you're not late to anything at all.

The fact that could even be possible dispels any notion that the asynchronous clock could be simply "information overload." What we have here is an illusion that presence is always behind, and relevance is always ahead. It tricks us into believing that to stay still is to disappear. But we're still there.

The thing is, we can stop scrolling, log off, even delete every account we have, and yet it would still be there. It's possible that we get disoriented because we do try shut it off when we're overwhelmed with it. Then, we're surprised when it doesn't stop. It's like trying to stop time.

Just as crossing time zones can desynchronize our internal clocks from the external environment, constant engagement with digital platforms can lead to a misalignment between our biological rhythms and the demands of the digital world. We were not designed to shift contexts, but that doesn't mean we can't.

CHAPTER TWENTY-ONE

Infusus

SUM OF THE PARTS

We've examined the importance of balance. But why bother? What could be the harm in a little mindless scrolling?

Toward the beginning of the book, we talked about a time when credibility was external. It came from the titles you carried, the credentials you held, the endorsements that flanked your name. You wore it like a uniform. People could glance in your direction and trust what they saw. We have already determined that time has passed. The signals are now mixed, the uniforms blurred. The cues are no longer reliable, and in some cases, they are superficial to the point of parody.

This shift created an opportunity. We now have a far more nuanced sense of worth, a far more democratic view of value, that is truer than it has ever been. We're now able to craft our own interior credibility without as many rigid markers placed upon us by ideologies that probably date back to World War II. Those systems rewarded uniformity, compliance, and appearances. What we're discovering now belongs to the individual, not the institution. It's something more personal. More portable. And far more resilient.

There is far more "you" to go around.

Navigating the new duality doesn't mean making less time for you. It actually means making more. You make the choice to live a balanced life, spending enough time within to curate your own, unique persona. Your reach, and your legacy expand exponentially.

Therefore, when coherence guides both presences, your inner alignment begins to shape your outer actions; not in mimicry, certainly not in rigid parallel, but in what I call *infusus*.

Infusus means that you carry one integrity, expressed two ways. By doing so, you live better. You make better decisions. Infusus doesn't need a script. Still, the contrast becomes clear when you see how it operates, versus the alternative.

Fig. 21:1 Infusus vs. Exterior Credibility
Dual selfhood as separate and fragmented vs. integrated and coherent.

INFUSUS	EXTERIOR CREDIBILITY
Seeks alignment	Seeks approval
Grounded in internal clarity	Grounded in visible status
Motivated by integrity	Motivated by optics
Comfortable with uncertainty	Overconfident in "certainty"
Speaks when ready to contribute	Speaks to be seen contributing
Self-assesses in carefully selected environments	Monitors self through feedback
Builds others' trust slowly through consistency	Gains attention quickly through self-promotion
Adapts	Ignores or reinvents
Can hold paradox	Needs to appear resolved
Creates meaning over time	Creates narrative in real time

Both the physical and digital realms have the illusion of moving faster than ever. So, we begin by determining where the physical and the digital self intersect. There, precisely where that convergence lives within us, we pause. You'll find that place within you surprisingly easy to locate. It is your most familiar self.

SYSTEMIC PRESSURE

While infusus definitely does begin with us looking within, it doesn't take place in stillness. It's a stabilizing force we carry with us, into the game. By now, we've recognized what is shared by our physical and our digital personas. We've reckoned with what isn't, and hopefully become comfortable with that, accepting that it's normal and natural. We accept that we will always operate in imperfect conditions in both realms, but that doesn't mean we can't stay grounded.

INFUSUS IN THE WILD

The best way to picture infusus is by interpreting it as the way we "walk" through the digital world. Physically, we might walk through an airport, then along a beach, hike up and down a mountain, return home and walk our child to school, go to work and walk through a massive parking lot and long hallways, to our desk. All walking, very different scenarios.

Vikas Jain and his colleagues empirically explored this further, noting how digital tools (such as GPS or calendar apps) act as cognitive scaffolding for navigating a consistent self in digital spaces, enhancing a narrative continuity much like walking connects physical locations.

Before you accuse me of oversimplifying this, know that is exactly my intention. As a toddler, we learned to walk. Figuratively, we need to do the same now in the digital realm. We've been idle, or crawling. We stay in one place or move very little in the overall awareness of ourselves as a digital being, a creator. We haven't been aware of the *need* to walk.

But we do need an awareness of the journey, effort and distance between our digital destinations, and that in-between does share a similarity with walking. It's a state. We assume that a toddler sees people walking. Developmentally, the young child is not capable of saying, "Those people can walk. I need to set a goal to achieve that, and work toward that goal." Instead, she just keeps working at it, and soon she takes her first steps.

The journey can be mundane, taxing, stressful, fun, relaxing… anything, really. Just like we can walk places, our digital whole is interconnected by the parts. As we move through the digital realm, we work toward interconnectedness. Awareness of that is really all we need.

Fig. 21:2 Navigating Digital Life
Without coherence, digital activity feels disconnected. But it isn't.

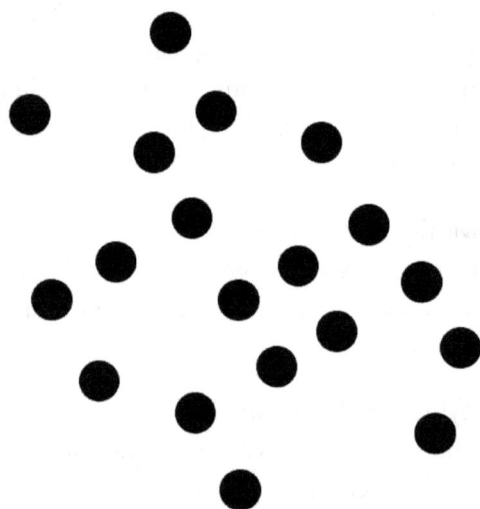

In this, figurative diagram of someone's day, each black dot represents an internet-related activity.

They wake, turn off the alarm on their phone, then check their notifications. They get out of bed and it's cold, but they're upstairs, and the thermostat is downstairs, so they use an app to turn on the heat, and turn it back off in an hour.

Downstairs, they sit and scroll the day's headlines for a minute, then check social media and pet the dog, who just ran out of food. On the way out the door, they order Starbucks, then check traffic and take the longer route to avoid construction, streaming a podcast while they drive.

At work, iced matcha latte in hand, they move between tabs in an ERP system, Slack, and spreadsheets. During lunch, they order groceries (including dog food) to be delivered between 6:00-7:00 to their doorstep.

Returning home after work, after feeding the dog of course, their evening consists of gaming on a console, texting, scrolling, calling their mom and streaming Netflix. Their phone is always nearby.

It looks like a random assortment of activities, because it is... but only in a sense.

Fig. 21:3 Navigating Digital Life with Infusus
Viewing our digital patterns as an existence, lived continuity.

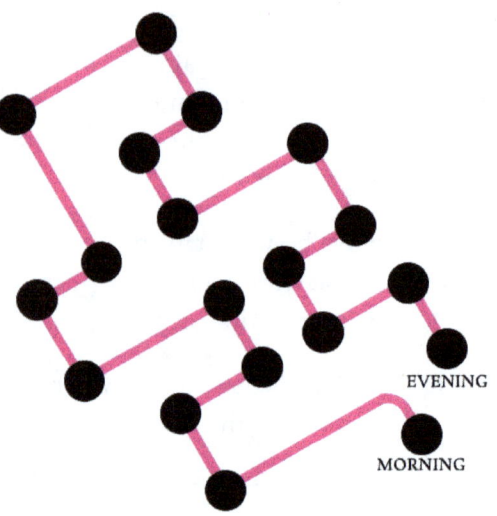

When the dots (your online activity) are connected by lines (using the analogy of digitally walking from one to the other), you are employing infusus. It's much easier to detect patterns. You're getting to know your digital self. That's coherence.

PART IV

BOTH OF ME

CHAPTER TWENTY-TWO
The New Authority

AUTHORITY DECOUPLED FROM HUMAN PRESENCE

We've talked about norms that have been upended by this new, dual world we are a part of. We've discussed brand new benchmarks for value and worth. But what about authority? Turns out, that has changed too. Even the word itself, *authority*, has a negative connotation now. But authority is often synonymous with important societal constructs like credibility and order. We need it.

This isn't your grandfather's authority. It isn't pretentious, domineering, or rooted in credentials. It doesn't pressure, compete for airtime, or demand obedience. It doesn't come from a podium or even a microphone. It runs quietly in the background.

For that reason, the new authority doesn't feel like authority at all, as we once knew it. It's a kind of presence that holds weight without force. Now, visibility confers power, and decisions don't require authorship or even consent.

During the 2008 financial crisis, some mortgage lenders used "robo-signing," where individuals electronically signed documents, including foreclosure paperwork, without verifying the information.

The practice, dubbed "rubber stamping," was used to process a large volume of foreclosures, leading to questionable practices and legal issues. People lost their homes, and the economy took one of the worst downturns of the era.

The 2010 Flash Crash erased nearly $1 trillion in minutes, caused by bots reacting recursively to one another's moves.

Today, fifteen years later, nobody questions it when algorithms decide financial futures.

Recommendation systems decide what knowledge is seen (e.g., Google, TikTok, Spotify).

Hiring algorithms and resume screening cause many qualified candidates to be filtered out before any human ever sees their name.

In travel, you're already evaluated now, before you arrive at the airport. Your proxy travels faster than you. Facial recognition in security at many airports, TSAPre, Clear, CBP's Global Entry, and eGates assess your risk level or identity before you speak to a human officer.

Content moderation is often performed at scale, with no human involvement. It may seem practical at first, but a growing divergent opinion that it is Orwellian or authoritarian has come from multiple sectors: scholars, journalists, ethicists, legal theorists, and even tech insiders. For example, in *Surveillance Capitalism*, Shoshana Zuboff critiques how platforms automate decision-making and normalize surveillance without transparency.

Zuboff's words, 'without transparency' are haunting. Who decides where the guardrails are? What are their qualifications to make assessments that impact human lives?

The new authority is not who speaks, but what the system listens to. There is a new "they." We used to say "they said it on the news." Now we say "I saw it online." But the "they" is ambient now. It's just a pattern that keeps appearing until we believe it.

"GOING VIRAL" ≠ "POPULAR"

We assume that if something goes viral, it was watched or reacted to a lot. A viral post appears to rise by public demand, but its momentum is shaped as much by system design as by human response. A viral post or reel can be, and often is, cyclical. Rewarded by itself. If it keeps showing up, the likelihood is that it will garner more watches and more positive reactions. That can easily be mistaken that for momentum. We then reward what has already been rewarded, and we can't reward what we never saw. That loop disguises itself as relevance.

WHAT RISES DOESN'T ALWAYS DO SO ON MERIT

In the digital world, most of what spreads quickly isn't what's most meaningful. When I discuss this topic with others, I find that it's difficult for people to accept. Many still would like to believe that what they care about is what matters most. If we're completely honest, the things that go viral are those which get the biggest reaction from an audience.

If you've ever swiped through multiple short-form videos, on your TikTok For You Page (FYP), Instagram of Facebook Reels, or YouTube Shorts, this is evident. You'll get a disjointed, unorganized mashup of topics, quality and relevance. Some will be hilarious. Others annoying. How did they get there? Not merit.

Legacy authority was once like a printed op-ed in the Sunday paper. You saw the credentials at the top, read the piece, and maybe nodded along. That was it. The author never had to defend their ideas in real time. Their authority came with the byline.

But Generation Z grew___ up in comment sections. They saw that authority didn't always hold when questioned. They watched experts get dismantled by people with better evidence or lived experience. They learned that tone, timing, and the ability to listen often mattered more than title or tenure.

In that space, authority wasn't randomly handed out. It had to hold up. If someone couldn't answer respectfully, admit gaps in their thinking, or engage with honesty, their voice didn't last. It didn't matter who they were.

As generation Z entered the workforce, authority became less about projection and more about presence. Less about being right and more about being real. Expect that trend to continue.

OUR AUTHORITY

Actually, the concept of crowdsourced, random authority is among the most positive aspects of the emergence of the internet. It reset society. One way we can tell is to assess authority in the physical realm. Multiple studies show that trust in traditional institutions (government, media, big business, policing) has declined significantly over the past two decades. Also that public trust in government and media in particular is at or near historic lows in the United States and similar patterns are observed globally.

The digital world has just as many flaws, if not more. Consider this widely-circulated meme:

"Don't believe everything you read on the internet just because there's a picture with a quote next to it."

- Abraham Lincoln

The same tools that elevate new voices can also amplify misinformation, polarization, even physical violence. What spreads isn't always what's coherent, just what's clickable. Still, the digital realm is arguably more democratic. The possibility of earned influence remains far more accessible.

What is liked, wins. It doesn't discriminate. "The man" has his presence, in that corporations own and operate portions of the web, but everyday citizens have a real voice, in a way they have never before. Open-source programs and Wikipedia, even Reddit, are examples of people who are not in a position of traditional authority, having an impact in powerful ways.

Despite its flaws there is a new town square, a global one, where a message can't be easily silenced and everyone can voice an opinion.

There was a time when authority could rely on insulation. Editors, publishers, and reputation acted as a buffer between the 'expert' and the crowd. That time is over. In today's digital environment, no platform is high enough to escape scrutiny. Comment sections, quote tweets, and online threads have become the new court of epistemic review, where anyone's claims can be dissected, corrected, or dismantled in real time. Expertise is no longer protected by title alone. What counts now is what survives the crowd.

Jonah Lehrer was a bestselling science writer whose credibility unraveled when readers and commenters began identifying fabricated quotes and recycled material. What began as informal online scrutiny quickly escalated into a full collapse of trust. His authority as a public intellectual was not taken by scandal, but revoked by the crowd.

Bari Weiss, formerly of *The New York Times*, launched her own publication, *Common Sense*, on Substack in 2021. It aimed to present "free-thinking" commentary outside of mainstream ideological constraints. Initially, the outlet gained traction, positioned as a counter to perceived institutional groupthink.

On several occasions, commenters on Twitter, Reddit, and Substack itself began pointing out factual slippages, cherry-picked sources, and misleading headlines or summaries of academic studies. All it took was a few high-traction threads, where regular commenters debunked her articles or pointed out how her arguments were distorted through selective framing.

Unlike a one-time scandal, credibility erosion happened in slow motion, through hundreds of public rebuttals and threads that challenged her reliability. Although it didn't destroy her audience, it did irrevocably fracture her credibility among moderates, many of whom had initially seen her as a needed alternative voice.

Even those with polished credentials or bestselling books must now pass through the gauntlet of distributed judgment, where regular people, armed with search bars and shared memory, determine what holds and what falls apart.

This shift in power does not stop with authors. Politicians, executives, influencers, and news anchors now operate under the same conditions of exposure. Their words are archived, replayed, and shared with comment by strangers who often know the subject better than they do.

Authority today is not declared, it is defended. Because of us.

CHAPTER TWENTY-THREE

The Independent Thinkers in the Room

STAYING ORIGINAL IN A SEA OF SYSTEM LOGIC

Up to now, we've taken a detailed look at the proxy condition. We've explored its evolution, examined misconceptions, risks and sociological conditions surrounding an unprecedented era already upon us. We have done quite a bit of then/now contrast to lay bare the unprecedented state we find ourselves in.

We've also studied the physical effect. Duality often being misconstrued as fatigue or attention deficit. Compulsion bordering addiction, and the dangers of becoming entrenched in either the physical or the digital realm in current-day society. We've spoken about acceptance. We are the first generations to exist this way.

The proxy condition will not end. Barring a societal collapse so severe that it places humanity back in the dark ages, it is here to stay. Unless you've been watching too many sci-fi movies, I think we can agree that Armageddon is not imminent.

Historically, the independent thinker was defined by resistance to conformity, and sometimes a willingness to hold unpopular opinions. This rebel, with or without a cause, operated against the system. Independence equaled being an outlier.

In the proxy era, independence no longer means isolation. The likelihood that just about anyone can find like-minded people in the digital realm is strong, no matter what their views are.

In addition to that, the system has become the universal tool for expression of ideas. It is well-documented that independent thinkers are responsible for a vast majority of the world's innovation, whether it be in science, philosophy or art. So, if independence itself has changed, what does that look like in today's world, where a five-year-old can produce a beautiful work of art?

There is not a way forward. There are *ways*. Not in the sense that there are choices (there are), but in the sense that we'll need to navigate *two*. At times, they will be in opposition to each other. That happens to me every night. My body wants to go to bed, but my digital self still has so much to do.

INTELLIGENCE IS EVOLVING

Fig. 23:1 A Musical Tuning Fork
Two tines, one vibration. Stability depends on staying in harmony with both states at once.

Left tine: The physical self.

Right tine: The digital self.

Center handle: Allows the pitch to be sustained.

The stability of the note that comes from a tuning fork is due to duality. According to Physics Stack Exchange, a tuning fork has two prongs to maintain a balanced, sustained vibration. When one prong vibrates, the other moves in the opposite direction, creating a balanced motion that prevents energy from being transferred to the holder (like your hand) and damping the vibration too quickly.

On a tuning fork, a sustained pitch is the product of both tines. The same is true today of our concept of intelligence. The person and the system both contribute. The system takes over where memory could potentially fail us, and does a lot of the dull work for us. We step in and build concepts within that scaffolding.

Fig. 23:2 The New Cognitive Caste System

In an automated world where systems can convincingly mimic expertise, taste, or content, traditional markers of intelligence become a baseline.

TRADITIONAL INTELLIGENCE (PRE-INTERNET ERA)	EXPANDED INTELLIGENCE (AI ERA)	THE NEW BASELINE
Memorization and recall	Judgment, intellectual creativity	Memory is nearly infinite. This opens up an entirely new realm of intelligence, while the importance of memorization and recall still remains crucial in many instances.
Fluent expression (writing/speaking)	Perspective and distinction	Literacy will never be irrelevant. Systems can compensate to some degree, but they cannot distinguish what matters or why.
Visual creativity	Narrative authorship	Output has become cheap. Vision tied to meaning is not. Intellectual creativity has expanded to mean artistic creativity as well.
Productivity or output volume	Intentional absence or curation	Output or volume used to be tied to hard work. Now, it is effortless. Editing has taken center stage.
Technical skill or fluency	Pattern awareness	Mastery of tools is no longer as rare, and in some cases unnecessary. Awareness of their framing is not.
Strategy and logic	Coherence	AI can simulate logic. Humans show intelligence through consistency and reflection.
Charisma or persona	Integrity across contexts	Identity curation is easy. Sustained alignment across contexts is rare.
Thought leadership	Originality	Systems can only extrapolate from what humans have input.
Local expertise	Instantaneous, global access	Local experts can use tools that extend their knowledge and they can retrieve them in real time.

FACT RECOLLECTION ≈ 100%

The digital world mirrors the physical one in its enormity. For that reason, assigning a single purpose to it is difficult. However, if we were to take a stab at it, we might borrow a term from the early days of the internet, when anyone who worked in the field was simply called "IT."

The abbreviation stands for "Information Technology." That title is fitting. Our digital selves are, in a sense, an extension of the brain. It is the *information* available to us that is transforming us, through technology.

One of the biggest differences between the physical and the digital realms is memory. Physical memory has limits. Digital memory does not.

Spelling bees used to be a thing. Although (I think) spelling bees are still around, knowing how to spell arcane words from memory doesn't have the same meaning it did in the 1950s.

Back then, if you wanted to impress grandma with your intelligence, you could just recite all the state capitals. Poor kids, the time they spent memorizing all of that stuff.

Somewhere along the way, we began to slowly realize that there was a lot more to intelligence than memory. In 1983, Howard Gardner's Theory of Multiple Intelligences gained wide notoriety for reframing intelligence as more than just IQ. His claim:

Being intelligent is not just solving math problems or remembering facts. It can mean understanding people (interpersonal), understanding yourself (intrapersonal), moving your body with precision (bodily-kinesthetic), or navigating space (spatial intelligence).

Then, along came the internet, and near-total-instant-recall became a given. With a connected device in front of us, we all have near-perfect memories now. Physical memory remains important, but this shift did create a new hierarchy for intelligence. Memory no longer equals wisdom. What once gave the impression of genius now gives the impression of *access*. To wit:

We all stepped one rung up on the cerebral ladder. With billions of facts always at our fingertips, being smart now means being intellectually creative, being an architect of ideas.

If he were alive today, Neil Postman may have perceived this as negative. It's possible he would have seen it as a flattening of intellectual hierarchy. That would be true if intellectual hierarchy were flat. But it isn't. Instead, we're in the midst of a meritocratic uprising of intellect, with thought leadership taking center stage.

If the AI era makes us all-knowing-adjacent, the baseline for many has shifted. The public now has tools once reserved for specialists. Everyone is a creator. The only true next-level thinkers will be those who can shape the paradigm itself.

At the same time, an attorney still needs to be able to instantly recollect case law without the use of a device. A doctor still needs to be able to recognize symptoms. This is duality, at its best.

MEMORY WITHOUT TIME

Traditional human memory is temporal. It fades, distorts, prioritizes emotionally salient details, and is co-authored by forgetting. It unfolds in a linear stream shaped by biological, narrative, and emotional logic.

Philosopher Bernard Stiegler warned that the industrialization of memory (through photography, then digital archives) creates a tertiary retention system. This means we rely on external systems to remember for us; Google, iCloud, Instagram archives, security footage, cached pages.

Maps has eliminated the necessity for us to remember routes. The knowledge would be useless anyway, since we can't factor in traffic conditions and road closures. We rely on systems to find the best route for us in real time.

Hiring platforms, scoring engines, and reputation indexes are structured to operate on memory traces.

To illustrate, let's assume there is a job applicant. In an analog scenario, he is seen leaving the interviewer's office by a co-worker. The co-worker steps into the interviewer's office after the applicant has left and says to the interviewer, "I recognize that guy. He used to be a neo-nazi in high school."

In the digital version of the story, a hiring algorithm locates a neo-nazi tweet that the applicant made in 2008, when he was in high school. The system reads the data as disqualifying, and the interview never takes place.

The difference in this instance: digital memory doesn't just shape judgment. It replaces it. The interviewer might have chosen to hire him anyway, but he is no longer the one making the decision, and it's exactly the type of decision that requires human logic to accurately make.

BROWSING IS AUTHORSHIP BY PROXY

Summing things up, in a world where production can be automated and expression mimicked, consumption is no longer passive. Every choice: what you click, scroll, view, share, save, or skip, is a contribution. It trains the proxy that speaks for you. It shapes the output.

We are the first generation to live this way. Our behaviors are no longer limited to creation or reaction. They are patterns of presence, of identity, and evidence of how we are being shaped. Consumption is no longer a neutral act. It builds the systems that will later reflect us back to ourselves. What we notice, what we choose, and what we ignore are no longer just habits. They are the early language of a new cognitive reality and a new temporal substrate. One that future generations will inherit without remembering a time before it.

Russell Belk's foundational work on the extended self in the digital world emphasizes how digital objects and interactions are not merely tools but extensions of identity, forming a "coherent self narrative" that responds to digital events

Not all consumption is the same. Some behaviors are deliberate. Others are automatic. Some center around thought. Others are tied to identity. The differences are subtle, but they matter. They all leave a trace.

Consumption can be categorized two ways; thought-oriented, and identity-oriented:

Thought-oriented Consumption

This kind of consumption shapes how we think, although we usually don't notice it. It is not defined by what we consume, but by the frame of mind we are in while doing it. It can strengthen pattern recognition, undermine attention, or create feedback loops that feel like thought but are only habit. Over time, it subtly alters how we approach information, how we problem-solve, and how we deal with uncertainty. It trains the mind to either settle, stretch, or avoid.

Identity-oriented Consumption

Here, the focus is not what we know, but what we are putting out there, even to ourselves. Every act of sharing, saving, posting, or scrolling becomes a kind of mirror. Identity-oriented consumption shapes the self as seen through systems; what we align with, what we resist, what we amplify. It often feels personal, but it is impression management, even when private. It can stabilize a sense of self or fracture it. Over time, it teaches us how to be seen, but not always how to know who we are.

PROXY FEEDBACK LOOP
(META-STRUCTURE ACROSS TWO AXES)

Digital behaviors are not isolated, singular actions. They're designed to make us think we're *just* clicking a video, or liking a post, or glancing at a news item. But every action is recorded, scored, and integrated.

It's essential to understand that recursive loop: the system reads what you do, adjusts what it shows you, and you respond again. What begins as a casual scroll becomes a pattern, then a persona. Thought-oriented behaviors influence identity. Identity-oriented actions feed back into how you think. The dynamic is invisible to you, but not to the system.

The danger is that, without awareness, feedback loops will be what trains your proxy self, conscious authorship on your part.

Fig. 23:3 Behavioral Axis I - Thought-oriented

In an automated world where systems can convincingly mimic expertise, taste, or content, traditional markers of intelligence become a baseline.

BEHAVIOR	DESCRIPTION	EXAMPLES
Organic	Occurs naturally, integrated with rhythm of life. You seek something, find it, exit. No dissonance or aftermath. Often, no viable alternate choice.	Checking your bank balance, looking up a recipe for dinner, reading an article you searched for, ordering a refill on a prescription, finding driving directions.
Compulsive	Triggered by stimulus or habit. You enter without intent, stay too long, and exit with reduced clarity or energy.	Social media, memes, games. Opening Instagram without realizing, watching reels, forgetting why you picked up your phone, cycling through apps when you're bored, playing a mobile game on autopilot.
Holistic	An extension of you, physically.	Talking to Alexa, using a fitness tracker as part of your routine, asking Siri to send a message while driving, checking your home camera feed for peace of mind.
Cerebral	Intellectual or educational.	Watching a documentary you sought out, completing a Duolingo lesson, looking up peer-reviewed research, reading longform journalism, taking an online course.
Entrained/ Recursive	The apps and devices you have chosen that become part of your daily life.	Checking email reflexively, your news feed. Anything associated with your employment (email, Slack, calendar).
Dissociative	Not emotionally regulated or intellectually engaged. Often passive, glazed, and trance-like.	Background autoplay, infinite feeds, binge-watching. Doomscrolling.

Fig. 23:4 Behavioral Axis II - Identity-oriented
Your proxy self is as much of a curated identity as your physical self, if not more.

BEHAVIOR	DESCRIPTION	EXAMPLES
Impression Management	The creation of a persona.	Social media accounts, avatars, screen names, blogs.
Reinforcement	Daily honing and realigning with your present self.	Posts, selfies, comments, likes, tags that reflect where you went, what you do, and what your current lifestyle is.
Expansion	A significant change in your persona.	Marriage, children, first-time major travel experiences, graduation, anything surrounding identity shifts, Coming out as LGBTQ+.
Displacement	Adopting frameworks or language that are borrowed/insincere.	Posting memes that don't represent your humor for likes/reactions, mimicking internet tone or slang, fake influencers.
Diluting	One of the hardest to detect. Constantly translating yourself for general audiences, overexplaining, or subtly editing thoughts to be palatable.	Dumbing down, suppressing personal opinions you feel your audience doesn't share, whitewashing, removing photos that capture you accurately, but don't fit your aesthetic.

We are the information, and it is us. To speak of "too much reliance" misses the point. It implies that the problem is quantity, when what we need is clarity. Checking your bank balance is not the same as compulsively cycling through apps. Social media presence is not inherently harmful, and face-to-face life is not immune to distortion. We can misrepresent ourselves anywhere.

The internet did not invent our shortcomings. It mirrored them.

Getting more granular in how we name these patterns helps us see more clearly. It removes the moral panic and replaces it with precision. This isn't about blaming the digital world. It's about learning to see it well enough to live inside it with discernment.

That is the work ahead; developing fluency in our actions and management of our digital selves. Because only then can we begin to shape it purposefully.

WHOLENESS

The digital realm is not inherently dangerous or soul-eroding any more than the physical world is. Both contain those elements, but neither can be defined as solely 'bad'.

You are not 'damaged' because you live in two realms. It's possible to be damaged while existing in either one. Problems will almost definitely arise if your digital identity is shaped without your awareness.

Intelligence has expanded in form, and self-expression comes from carrying your values across both realities with intention.

This is the new expression of wholeness.

So, what are the conditions for becoming whole when systems structure perception, participation, and possibility before the self is even formed?

Wholeness in the proxy condition emerges at the intersection of intention and infrastructure, between what we feel and how systems respond.

In physical development, wholeness follows a sequence of needs. In the proxy condition, it begins with awareness of systemic mediation.

Stiegler argued, technical systems exteriorize memory and perception, restructuring not only how identity is formed but when it begins.

System-aware selfhood is when the part of your identity that emerges across conditions of partial legibility *remains intact* because you are the one coordinating it.

This echoes the philosopher Judith Butler's insight that to be rendered visible as a subject is always to be filtered through frames of legibility that precede and constrain what the self can be. Wholeness in both realms is achieved and maintained because it is managed, not because it is granted.

Infusus, in the proxy condition, is the continuity of values, agency, and presence across two separate architectures that do not share a common frame for interpreting the self.

To be whole now is to remain internally aligned while navigating systems that cannot agree on what you are.

AI DIDN'T REPLACE YOU AFTER ALL?

Let me be clear. Artificial intelligence will eliminate some jobs. It will realign others. That is not new. Technology has always redrawn the boundaries of work.

In the 1940s, entire rooms were filled with typists. Mostly women. They created documents by hand, one at a time. Then came the photocopier. Almost overnight, the work was gone. Xerox executives became millionaires. The typists did not

Fig. 23:5 A typical 1940s secretarial pool.

Until the photocopier was invented and they were all out of a job.

According to the U.S. Bureau of Labor Statistics, secretarial and typing jobs fell by more than sixty percent between 1980 and 2020. The decline began earlier than most realize. Other technologies followed. The mainframe. The fax machine. Answering machines. Reception desks emptied out. Document couriers vanished. The economy adjusted. But people were left behind.

As an author, I'm aware of the risk. It would be naïve to suggest otherwise Mine is one of the professions potentially on the chopping block. But the fear that artificial intelligence would take our jobs was always shaped by a doomsday-oriented assumption, bolstered by for-profit media that leverages our fears to sell ads. The false premise here imagines that the value of work lies in the task. In the output. That once the task are gone, so is the person. In the capitalist structure we've created, those are the "measurables".

And yes, some of us will have to pivot, and the cost might be substantial.

But assuming that AI will render the human being's contribution useless is a narrow view of what work really is. Defined that way, you wouldn't be reading this. I'd be on unemployment. It's a good thing the act of arranging words is not all that makes someone a writer.

AI took the part of the job that can be mimicked. That can look like skill from a distance, like output.

What it didn't take is the part that makes the work matter.

It didn't take away your judgment, or your ability to sense what is missing. You still possess an ability to detect a misunderstanding, an ability to immediately see that something is off or missing, that AI can't match.

Machines are more complex than we are in scale, speed, and raw calculation. Humans are more complex in architecture, awareness, and adaptability.

The human remains unmatched in the kind of presence that feels, interprets, and acts with meaning.

If you don't believe that, try a text-to-image generator. Be as specific as you can. You might get something close. You might not. It will improve, but it will never completely know what you meant. It will never know the part of the image you didn't describe because you assumed it was obvious. It will never be perfect. Here's why.

Systems can do the work. But they can't care that it gets done. They cannot carry the weight of why it matters. They can't tell which email should be answered first, and which one can wait. They can't feel urgency when the stakes are rising. They will not be held accountable when things go wrong.

Systems can only output, and iterate what is already there, but we will always need new ideas, creativity and insight.

They can predict trends, but not the perfect storm of public mood, current events and even natural disasters that make some trends endure and others fade.

They can't tell when they're stating the obvious, or when they've said something obviously false.

They can simulate creativity. But they can't be moved by it. They can make a collage. But they can't decide what not to include. They can't feel the risk in a decision. Or the cost of getting it wrong.

Give AI an equal number of valid inputs from both sides of an argument. It won't know which side should hold. It won't know what matters most when everything looks equally plausible. It won't know which details are expendable and which ones are sacred.

In short, systems don't carry stakes. They don't infer what's unsaid. They don't hold authorship or ownership, only execution. They don't grieve, regret, or realign based on lived experience. They can't feel bad, or good.

Lastly, systems will never be able to simply iterate a "you." As far as physical humans are concerned, there is no "old" in the sense of being passé. No obsolescence. Only new.

Systems run only when we run them. We're running this one.

I OWE YOU A BEER

Figuratively, I actually don't drink beer :)

The one who asked me the one question that blew my mind. You know who you are.

For the one who wouldn't be ignored. The one who said aloud what everyone else was thinking. For the one who made all of us laugh. The one who was actually energized by being proven wrong.

For the one who brought food on the late nights. For Tylenol on ten-hour days. Those who jumped right in the minute they heard about this project. You, who rolled your eyes, but stayed patient while I explained my concept. You understood in the end, and respected it, which was what made me believe I could move forward with this manuscript.

For those of you who get what it's like to be an indie author, and know that we don't have large publishing houses to back us or promote our work. Who know that if this story reaches new readers, it will be because someone like you felt like it was worth passing on.

For whatever brought you here, you're the reason this exists. You have my gratitude.

ABOUT THE AUTHOR'S PHYSICAL SELF

Harrison Rose Tate is a systems thinker, technologist, and author whose work explores the intersection of cognition, philosophy, culture, and code. With a professional background in IT leadership, system architecture, and organizational strategy, she brings firsthand insight into the recursive logic of the digital world and its effects on human identity, presence, and autonomy.

Her extensive career over the last two decades as a writer has largely been on behalf of corporations, often without a byline. Her work has appeared in essays, articles, technical publications, and archival formats. Her academic background includes a master's degree, but most of her insight comes from years spent inside the system; building it, running it, watching how it shapes the people who use it. After years of ghostwriting, consulting, and building systems for others, **The Proxy Condition** has special meaning, as the first major work released in her own name.

Tate has lived and traveled extensively throughout the world. The research and authoring of this book spanned place and time. The result is a true cultural artifact, reframing how we think about presence, autonomy, and meaning in the digital age. Fierce and calculated all at once, it doesn't back down from the questions most people are just beginning to ask.

SOURCE CODE

AI Image Generators (DALL·E 2, Midjourney, Stable Diffusion). 2022. Referenced in general coverage of generative image AI. See: Heaven, Will. 2022. "AI-Generated Art Is Here, and the World Is Already Different." *MIT Technology Review*. https://www.technologyreview.com/2022/10/19/1061370

AIA – Advancing Vision + Imaging. "Understanding Vision Systems in High-Speed Production Lines." *Automate.org*. Accessed May 26, 2025. https://www.automate.org/vision/articles/understanding-vision-systems-in-high-speed-production-lines

Allied Market Research. "Ambient Intelligence Market Size & Share Analysis." Accessed May 2025. https://www.alliedmarketresearch.com/ambient-intelligence-market

Amazon. "Our History." Accessed May 2025. https://www.aboutamazon.com/our-company/history

Amazon. "Meet Alexa." Amazon. Accessed April 2025. https://www.amazon.com/alexa

Amazon.com. 2007. "Introducing Amazon Kindle." Accessed May 2025. https://www.amazon.com/b?node=1268192011

Amiot, Catherine E., Roxane de la Sablonnière, Danielle Jetté, and Simon M. Smith. "Integration of Social Identities in the Self: Toward a Cognitive-Developmental Model." *Personality and Social Psychology Review* 11, no. 4 (2007): 364–388. https://doi.org/10.1177/1088868307304091

Andrews-Hanna, Jessica R., R. Nathan Spreng, Jonathan R. Eisenberg, and R. Todd Braver. "The Default Network and Self-Generated Thought: Component Processes, Dynamic Control, and Clinical Relevance." *Annals of the New York Academy of Sciences* 1316, no. 1 (2014): 29–52. https://doi.org/10.1111/nyas.12360

AnonymousCarrot. 2025. "/TrueOffMyChest." *Reddit*. https://www.reddit.com

Apple Inc. 2007. "Apple Reinvents the Phone with iPhone." Press release, January 9, 2007. https://www.apple.com/newsroom/2007/01/09Apple-Reinvents-the-Phone-with-iPhone

Apple Inc. 2008. "Apple Launches the App Store." Press release, July 10, 2008. https://www.apple.com/newsroom/2008/07/10Apple-Launches-the-App-Store

Armstrong, David M. *A World of States of Affairs* (Cambridge: Cambridge University Press, 1997), 41.

Ashforth, Blake E., Glen E. Kreiner, and Mel Fugate. "All in a Day's Work: Boundaries and Micro Role Transitions." *Academy of Management Review* 25, no. 3 (2000): 472–491. https://doi.org/10.5465/amr.2000.3363315

Bahaghighat, M., Abedini, F., and S'hoyan, M. "Vision Inspection of Bottle Caps in Drink Factories Using Convolutional Neural Networks." *IEEE*, 2019. https://www.researchgate.net/publication/334786229

Beckhoff Automation. "Quality Control with Vision Systems in Beverage Bottling." *Beckhoff USA Blog*, 2023. https://www.beckhoff.com/en-us/company/news/beverage-bottling-vision

Beeple. 2021. *Everydays: The First 5000 Days*. Digital artwork. Sold via Christie's, March 11, 2021. Accessed May 2025. https://onlineonly.christies.com/s/everydays-first-5000-days

Stiegler, Bernard. *Technics and Time, 1: The Fault of Epimetheus*. Translated by Richard Beardsworth and George Collins. Stanford: Stanford University Press, 1998.

Blogger.com. "History of Blogger." Accessed May 2025. https://blogger.googleblog.com/2008/08/10-years-of-blogger.html

Britannica. "Johannes Gutenberg and the Printing Press." Accessed May 2025. https://www.britannica.com/biography/Johannes-Gutenberg

Brooklyn Nine-Nine. 2013–2021. Created by Dan Goor and Michael Schur. Performances by Andre Braugher and Andy Samberg. NBC.

Business of Fashion. 2020. "The Streetwear Report." *Business of Fashion Insights*. Accessed May 2025. https://www.businessoffashion.com/articles/intelligence/streetwear-report-2020

Carr, Nicholas. The Shallows: What the Internet Is Doing to Our Brains. New York: W. W. Norton & Company, 2010.

Carvana. 2024. "How Carvana Works." Accessed May 2025. https://www.carvana.com/how-it-works

Chayka, Kyle. *Filterworld: How Algorithms Flattened Culture*. New York: Doubleday, 2024.

Cognex Corporation. "How AI and Machine Vision Improve Pharmaceutical Product Quality and Yield." *Cognex Blog*, April 2023. https://www.cognex.com/blogs/machine-vision/how-ai-and-machine-vision-improve-pharmaceutical-product-quality-and-yield

Confessore, Nicholas. 2018. "Cambridge Analytica and Facebook: The Scandal and the Fallout So Far." *New York Times*, April 4, 2018. https://www.nytimes.com/2018/04/04/us/politics/cambridge-analytica-scandal.html

da Silva, F. P., Jerónimo, H. M., and Henriques, P. L. "Impact of Digital Burnout on the Use of Digital Consumer Platforms." *Technological Forecasting and Social Change*, 2024.

Derrida, Jacques. "Plato's Pharmacy." In *Dissemination*, translated by Barbara Johnson, 61–171. Chicago: University of Chicago Press, 1981.

Dickens, Charles. 1859. *A Tale of Two Cities*. London: Chapman & Hall.

Duolingo. "Duolingo Now Powered by AI: Educators Reimagined." *Duolingo Newsroom*, February 6, 2025. https://blog.duolingo.com/ai-teaching-shift

Eagles. "Hotel California." *Hotel California*. Asylum Records, 1976. Written by Don Felder, Don Henley, and Glenn Frey.

eBay Inc. "Company History." Accessed May 2025. https://www.ebayinc.com/our-company/our-history

Eilish, Billie. 2024. "Billie Eilish Compares Her Frequent Social Media Usage to Smoking Cigarettes." *People*, February 21, 2024. https://people.com/billie-eilish-compares-her-frequent-social-media-usage-to-smoking-cigarettes-8756955

Entertainment Software Association. 2013. "2013 Essential Facts About the Computer and Video Game Industry." Accessed May 2025. https://www.theesa.com/wp-content/uploads/2024/02/2013-EF-FINAL.pdf

Eriksen, Thomas Hylland. *Tyranny of the Moment: Fast and Slow Time in the Information Age*. London: Pluto Press, 2001.

European Union. "Regulation (EU) 2016/679 of the European Parliament and of the Council of 27 April 2016." *Official Journal of the European Union*, May 4, 2016. Accessed May 2025. https://eur-lex.europa.eu/eli/reg/2016/679/oj

Facebook. 2007. "Facebook Platform." Accessed May 2025. https://developers.facebook.com/docs/platform

Facebook. 2009. "Introducing the Like Button." Accessed May 2025. https://about.fb.com/news/2009/02/introducing-the-facebook-like-button

Facebook. 2012. "Timeline: A New Way to Express Who You Are." *Meta Newsroom*. Accessed May 2025. https://about.fb.com/news/2011/09/timeline-a-new-way-to-express-who-you-are

Farhangi, O., and Sheidaee, E. "Machine Vision for Detecting Defects in Liquid Bottles: An Industrial Application for Food and Packaging Sector." *Clean Energy and Clean Design Solutions* 5, no. 2 (2024). https://app.scholarai.io/paper?paper_id=DOI:10.37256/ccds.5220244756

Federal Communications Commission. *Enhanced 9-1-1 (E911)*. Accessed May 26, 2025. https://transition.fcc.gov/hspc/factsheets/enhanced911.pdf

Federal Communications Commission. *Wireless 911 Service*. Accessed May 26, 2025. https://www.fcc.gov/consumers/guides/wireless-911-service

Förster, Yves. "The Hyperconnected Now: Rethinking Time in the Digital Age." *World Economic Forum*, March 3, 2022. https://www.weforum.org/agenda/2022/03/the-hyperconnected-now

FujiFilm. "Digital Camera Evolution." Accessed May 2025. https://www.fujifilm.com/about/technology/digital_cameras

Garmin. "The History of GPS Navigation." Accessed May 2025. https://www.garmin.com/en-US/blog/general/the-history-of-gps-navigation

General Motors. 2009. "OnStar Turns 13 and Adds New Features." Accessed May 2025. https://media.gm.com/media/us/en/onstar/news.detail.html/content/Pages/news/us/en/2009/Jun/0602_onstar.html

Geocities. "Welcome to GeoCities." *Internet Archive Snapshot*, 1996. Accessed May 2025. https://web.archive.org/web/19961017235955/http://www.geocities.com/

Ghostwriter. 2023. "Heart on My Sleeve." *TikTok*. Accessed May 2025. [Song imitating Drake and The Weeknd using AI, later removed.]

GoFundMe. 2010. "About Us." *GoFundMe*. Accessed May 2025. https://www.gofundme.com/about-us

Gomez, Selena. 2023. "Selena Gomez on Mental Health, Instagram Fame, and Why She Left Social Media." *Vanity Fair*, February 15, 2023. https://www.vanityfair.com/style/2023/02/selena-gomez-takes-social-media-break-too-old-for-this-most-followed-person-instagram-kylie-jenner

Google. "Our History." Accessed May 2025. https://about.google/intl/en/our-story

Google. 2008. "A Fresh Take on the Browser: Introducing Google Chrome." Accessed May 2025. https://blog.google/products/chrome/introducing-google-chrome

Grand View Research. *Wearable Technology Market Size, Share & Trends Analysis Report By Product (Wrist-wear, Eye-wear & Head-wear, Foot-wear), By Application, By Region, And Segment Forecasts, 2024–2030.* San Francisco: Grand View Research, 2024. https://www.grandviewresearch.com/industry-analysis/wearable-technology-market

Greenwald, Glenn. 2013. "NSA Collecting Phone Records of Millions of Verizon Customers Daily." *The Guardian*, June 5, 2013. https://www.theguardian.com/world/2013/jun/06/nsa-phone-records-verizon-court-order

Griffey, Harriet. "We're All Distracted All the Time – Can Digital Detoxing Fix It?" *The Guardian*, May 16, 2018. https://www.theguardian.com/lifeandstyle/2018/may/16/we-are-all-distracted-all-the-time-can-digital-detoxing-fix-it

GSMA Intelligence. 2024. "The Mobile Economy 2024." Accessed May 2025. https://www.gsma.com/mobileeconomy

Haidt, Jonathan. *The Righteous Mind: Why Good People Are Divided by Politics and Religion.* New York: Vintage Books, 2012.

Han, Byung-Chul. The Transparency Society. Translated by Erik Butler. Stanford, CA: Stanford University Press, 2015.

Hao, Karen. 2025. "AI Governance Tools Are Here—But Do They Work?" *MIT Technology Review*, March 18, 2025. https://www.technologyreview.com/2025/03/18/ai-governance-tools

Harris, Bethan. 2022. "Ruby Franke Arrested: What We Know About the Influencer Mom's Case." *People*, December 1, 2022. https://people.com/ruby-franke-arrested-influencer-mom-case-8359231

Hatano, Yoshiro. 1993. "Use of the Pedometer for Promoting Daily Walking Exercise." *International Council for Health, Physical Education, and Recreation*, vol. 29.

Haugen, Frances. 2021. "Testimony Before the United States Senate." *U.S. Senate Subcommittee on Consumer Protection, Product Safety, and Data Security*, October 5, 2021. https://www.commerce.senate.gov/2021/10/protecting-kids-online-testimony-by-frances-haugen

Horwitz, Jeff. 2021. "The Facebook Files." *Wall Street Journal*, September 13, 2021. https://www.wsj.com/articles/the-facebook-files-11631713039

Instagram. 2010. "Instagram Launches." Accessed May 2025. https://about.instagram.com/blog/announcements/instagram-launches

International Labour Organization. *World Employment and Social Outlook: Trends 2021*. Geneva: ILO, 2021.

International Telecommunication Union (ITU). 2024. "Facts and Figures 2024: Measuring Digital Development." Accessed May 2025. https://www.itu.int/en/ITU-D/Statistics/Pages/facts/default.aspx

Isaac, Mike, and Kate Conger. 2022. "Elon Musk Completes $44 Billion Deal to Own Twitter." *New York Times*, October 27, 2022. https://www.nytimes.com/2022/10/27/technology/elon-musk-twitter-sale.html

Butler, Judith. *Frames of War: When Is Life Grievable?* London: Verso, 2009.

Kaur, Sandeep, and M. V. Raghunadh. "A Survey on Vision-Based Quality Control for Food and Beverage Packaging." *Procedia Computer Science* 167 (2020): 253–262. https://doi.org/10.1016/j.procs.2020.03.221

Kemp, Simon. 2024. "Digital 2024: Global Overview Report." *DataReportal*. https://datareportal.com/reports/digital-2024-global-overview-report

Kleon, Austin. 2012. *Steal Like an Artist*. New York: Workman Publishing.

Lee, I-Min, et al. 2011. "Step Definitions and Their Effects on Monitoring Physical Activity." *Journal of Obesity*, vol. 2011.

Lenovo. "Lenovo Uses AI to Transform Customer Experience and Supply Chain." *Lenovo StoryHub*, June 14, 2023. https://news.lenovo.com/news/lenovo-ai-customer-supply-chain

Leskin, Paige. 2019. "TikTok, the Short-Video App Gen Z Loves, Explained." *Business Insider*, July 17, 2019. https://www.businessinsider.com/what-is-tiktok-guide

Lieberman, Philip. 2007. "The Evolution of Human Speech: Its Anatomical and Neural Bases." *Current Anthropology* 48(1): 39–66. https://doi.org/10.1086/509092

LiveJournal. "LiveJournal History." Accessed May 2025. https://www.livejournal.com/about

Match Group. "Match.com: Our Story." Accessed May 2025. https://mtch.com/our-story

McKinsey & Company. 2021. "The State of Fashion 2021." Accessed May 2025. https://www.mckinsey.com/industries/retail/our-insights/state-of-fashion

McLuhan, Marshall. 1964. *Understanding Media: The Extensions of Man*. New York: McGraw-Hill.

Men's Fitness. 2007. "Andy Roddick Cover Controversy." Archived issue, August 2007.

Metz, Cade. "A.I. Is Changing How Walmart Delivers Online Orders." *New York Times*, March 7, 2023. https://www.nytimes.com/2023/03/07/technology/walmart-robotic-warehouses.html

Microsoft. 2025. "Microsoft Makes Major Leap in Quantum Computing with First Error-Corrected Qubit." *Microsoft Blog*, March 4, 2025. https://blogs.microsoft.com/blog/2025/03/04/microsoft-makes-major-leap-in-quantum-computing-with-first-error-corrected-qubit

Midjourney. 2022. "AI-Generated Images: Creativity at Scale." *Midjourney Showcase*. Accessed May 2025. https://www.midjourney.com/showcase

Mordor Intelligence. "Ambient Intelligence Market – Growth, Trends, Forecasts (2025–2032)." Accessed May 2025. https://www.mordorintelligence.com/industry-reports/ambient-intelligence

Morozov, Evgeny. To Save Everything, Click Here: The Folly of Technological Solutionism. New York: PublicAffairs, 2013.

Nakamoto, Satoshi. 2009. "Bitcoin: A Peer-to-Peer Electronic Cash System." https://bitcoin.org/bitcoin.pdf

Napster. "The Rise and Fall of Napster." *Internet Archive Snapshot*, 2001. Accessed May 2025. https://web.archive.org/web/20011126141800/http://www.napster.com

Nepal, Surya, Juan Hernandez, Rhys Lewis, and Ahsan Chaudhry. "Burnout in Cybersecurity Incident Responders: Exploring the Factors That Light the Fire." *ACM Digital Library*, 2024. https://dl.acm.org/doi/abs/10.1145/3637304

Nest Labs. 2010. "Nest Learning Thermostat." Accessed May 2025. https://nest.com

Netscape Communications. "Secure Sockets Layer (SSL) Protocol." *Netscape Developer Documentation Archive*, 1994. Accessed May 2025. https://web.archive.org/web/19970121183352/http://home.netscape.com/info/security-doc.html

Newport, Cal. 2019. *Digital Minimalism: Choosing a Focused Life in a Noisy World*. New York: Portfolio.

Niantic. "Pokémon GO." *Pokémon Company International*, July 6, 2016. https://www.pokemongolive.com

Norman, Don. *The Design of Everyday Things*. Revised and Expanded Edition. New York: Basic Books, 2013.

Odell, Jenny. 2019. *How to Do Nothing: Resisting the Attention Economy*. Brooklyn, NY: Melville House.

OpenAI. "Introducing ChatGPT." *OpenAI Blog*, November 30, 2022. https://openai.com/blog/chatgpt

—— 2022. "ChatGPT Research Release." *OpenAI*, November 30, 2022. https://openai.com/blog/chatgpt

—— 2022. "ChatGPT." *OpenAI.com*. Accessed May 2025. https://chat.openai.com

Oxford Languages. 2013. "Oxford Dictionaries Word of the Year 2013." *Oxford University Press*. Accessed May 2025. https://languages.oup.com/word-of-the-year/2013

——. 2015. "Oxford Dictionaries Word of the Year 2015." *Oxford University Press*. Accessed May 2025. https://languages.oup.com/word-of-the-year/2015

Packaging Strategies. "Vision System Enables Traceability and Authentication for Pharmaceutical Manufacturers." *Packaging Strategies*, March 2021. https://www.packagingstrategies.com/articles/88270-vision-system-enables-traceability-and-authentication-for-pharmaceutical-manufacturers

Park, Randall. 2024. "Randall Park Says Social Media Contributed to Panic Attacks, So He Quit for Good." *People*, March 26, 2024. https://people.com/randall-park-suffered-back-to-back-panic-attacks-before-quitting-social-media-exclusive-11705470

PayPal. "History of PayPal." Accessed May 2025. https://newsroom.paypal-corp.com/history

Peele, Jordan. "You Won't Believe What Obama Says In This Video!" *YouTube*, April 17, 2018. Accessed May 2025. https://www.youTube.com/watch?v=cQ54GDm1eL0

Pew Research Center. 2008. "The Internet and the 2008 Election." Accessed May 2025. https://www.pewresearch.org/internet/2008/06/15/the-internet-and-the-2008-election

— 2010. "Cell Phones and American Adults." Accessed May 2025. https://www.pewresearch.org/internet/2010/09/02/cell-phones-and-american-adults

— 2023. "How Gen Z Sees Their Identity." Accessed May 2025. https://www.pewresearch.org/social-trends/2023/08/15/how-gen-z-sees-their-identity

— 2023. "Teens, Social Media and Technology 2023." Accessed May 2025. https://www.pewresearch.org/internet/2023/12/11/teens-social-media-and-technology-2023

Physics Stack Exchange. "What Is Heard When a Tuning Fork Is Struck?" *Physics Stack Exchange*, January 24, 2023. https://physics.stackexchange.com/questions/748292/what-is-heard-when-a-tuning-fork-is-struck

Pinkerton, Brian. 1994. "Introducing WebCrawler." *University of Washington*. Accessed May 2025. https://www.searchenginehistory.com/webcrawler

The Police. 1983. "Every Breath You Take." *Synchronicity*. A&M Records.

Postman, Neil. 1985. *Amusing Ourselves to Death: Public Discourse in the Age of Show Business*. New York: Viking Penguin.
— *Technopoly: The Surrender of Culture to Technology*. New York: Vintage Books.

Puértolas, Romain. 2014. *The Extraordinary Journey of the Fakir Who Got Trapped in an Ikea Wardrobe*. London: Harvill Secker.

Raichle, Marcus E. "The Brain's Default Mode Network." *Annual Review of Neuroscience* 38 (2015): 433–447. https://doi.org/10.1146/annurev-neuro-071013-014030

Ray Tomlinson. "The First Network Email." Accessed May 2025. https://www.raytomlinson.com

Reddit user. "Why Does Entertainment on the Internet Make Me Tired?" *r/nosurf* (Reddit), May 2025. https://www.reddit.com/r/nosurf

Reinecke, Leonard. "Media Multitasking and Well-Being: A Review and Synthesis of the Literature." *Computers in Human Behavior* 72 (2017): 315–324. https://doi.org/10.1016/j.chb.2017.03.048

Reiner, Rob, director. 1987. *The Princess Bride*. Performance by Wallace Shawn (Vizzini). Twentieth Century Fox.

ReviseSociology. "Information Overload and the Fragmentation of Attention." *ReviseSociology.com*, January 9, 2021. https://revisesociology.com/2021/01/09/information-overload-fragmented-attention

RIAA. "RIAA v. People: Four Years Later." Accessed May 2025. https://www.riaa.com/resources-learning

Rockwell Automation. "AI-Powered Quality Control is Changing Manufacturing." *RockwellAutomation.com*. Accessed May 26, 2025. https://www.rockwellautomation.com/en-us/company/news/blogs/ai-quality-control.html

SAG-AFTRA and WGA Strikes. 2023. "Actors and Writers Strike Over AI Likeness and Compensation." *The Hollywood Reporter*, July 2023. https://www.hollywoodreporter.com/business/business-news/sag-aftra-strike-wga-hollywood-1235537370

Sardar, Ziauddin. "Postnormal Times Revisited." *Journal of Futures Studies* 25, no. 3 (2021): 61–80. https://jfsdigital.org/articles-and-essays/2021-2/vol-25-no-3-march/postnormal-times-revisited

Settles, Isis H. "When Multiple Identities Interfere: The Role of Identity Centrality." *Personality and Social Psychology Bulletin* 30, no. 4 (2004): 487–500. https://doi.org/10.1177/0146167203261885

Sheeran, Ed. 2025. "Ed Sheeran Slams Reports That He Attended J.K. Rowling's New Year's Eve Party." *People*, January 3, 2025. https://people.com/ed-sheeran-slams-reports-that-he-attended-jk-rowlings-new-years-eve-party-8778432

Shuangyang, Z. "Fast Inspection of Food Packing Seals Using Machine Vision." *IEEE*, 2010. https://ieeexplore.ieee.org/abstract/document/5701262

Siegel, Daniel J. 2020. *The Developing Mind: How Relationships and the Brain Interact to Shape Who We Are*. 3rd ed. New York: Guilford Press.

Slack Technologies. 2020. *Slack*. Accessed May 2025. https://slack.com

Snap Inc. 2011. "*Snapchat: The Fastest Way to Share a Moment.*" Accessed May 2025. https://www.snapchat.com

Snapes, Laura. 2023. "AI Song Featuring Fake Drake and Weeknd Vocals Pulled from Streaming Services." *The Guardian*, April 18, 2023. Accessed May 2025. https://www.theguardian.com/music/2023/apr/18/ai-song-featuring-fake-drake-and-weeknd-vocals-pulled-from-streaming-services

Stable Diffusion. 2022. "Stable Diffusion by Stability AI." *GitHub Repository*. https://github.com/CompVis/stable-diffusion

Sontag, Susan. On Photography. New York: Farrar, Straus and Giroux, 1977.

Star Trek: The Next Generation. 1989. "The Best of Both Worlds, Part I." Season 3, Episode 26. Directed by Cliff Bole. Paramount Television.

Stern, Jessica. "Why Digital Time Feels Different." *Psychology Today*, April 11, 2022. https://www.psychologytoday.com/us/blog/rewired-the-psychology-of-tech/202204/why-digital-time-feels-different

Stiegler, Bernard. *Technics and Time, 1: The Fault of Epimetheus*. Translated by Richard Beardsworth and George Collins. Stanford, CA: Stanford University Press, 1998.

Symantec Corporation. "The History of Norton Antivirus." Accessed May 2025. https://www.nortonlifelock.com/company/history

The Numbers. 2013. "Top 2013 Movies at the Worldwide Box Office." Accessed May 2025. https://www.the-numbers.com/box-office-records/worldwide/all-movies/cumulative/released-in-2013

throwaway84112788221. "/TrueOffMyChest." *Reddit*, 2025. https://www.reddit.com

TikTok. 2019. *TikTok*. Accessed May 2025. https://www.tiktok.com

Tinder. 2012. "Swipe Life: Our Story." *Tinder*. Accessed May 2025. https://www.gotinder.com/about

Tolle, Eckhart. 1999. *The Power of Now: A Guide to Spiritual Enlightenment*. Novato, CA: New World Library.

Tor Project. "Overview of the Tor Project." Accessed May 2025. https://www.torproject.org/about/history/

Tudor-Locke, Catrine, et al. 2011. "How Many Steps/Day Are Enough? For Adults." *International Journal of Behavioral Nutrition and Physical Activity* 8, no. 1.

Turkle, Sherry. 2011. *Alone Together: Why We Expect More from Technology and Less from Each Other*. New York: Basic Books.
— 2015. *Reclaiming Conversation: The Power of Talk in a Digital Age*. New York: Penguin Books.

Turnitin. "AI Writing Detection Capabilities." *Turnitin*, 2023. https://www.turnitin.com

Twitter. 2009. "Twitter as a News Source." Accessed May 2025. https://blog.twitter.com/en_us/a/2009/twitter-and-news

U.S. Department of Labor. "Employment Situation Summary – April 2025." *U.S. Bureau of Labor Statistics*, May 2025.

U.S. Food and Drug Administration. *Drug Supply Chain Security Act (DSCSA)*. Updated April 2023. https://www.fda.gov/drugs/drug-supply-chain-integrity/drug-supply-chain-security-act-dscsa

Uber. 2009. "Our Story." Accessed May 2025. https://www.uber.com/us/en/about

United Nations Department of Economic and Social Affairs, Population Division. *World Population Prospects 2024: Summary of Results*. United Nations, 2024.

United Nations. 2025. "Global AI Governance Efforts Begin to Take Shape." Accessed May 2025. https://www.un.org/en/global-issues/artificial-intelligence

United States Senate. 2017. "Russian Interference in the 2016 Election." *Senate Intelligence Committee*. https://www.intelligence.senate.gov/publications/russian-interference-2016-election

University of Washington. 1994. "WebCrawler Launches First Full-Text Search Engine." Accessed May 2025. https://www.searchenginehistory.com/webcrawler

Vick, Karl. 2015. "The Ashley Madison Hack: What You Need to Know." *Time*, August 19, 2015. https://time.com/4002821/ashley-madison-hack-explained

Vincent, James. "AI-Generated Image of Pope Wearing Puffer Coat Goes Viral." *The Verge*, March 27, 2023. https://www.theverge.com/2023/3/27/pope-puffer-coat-ai-image-deepfake

Vincent, James. "ChatGPT Took the World by Storm. Here's What We Know About Its Launch." *The Verge*, December 1, 2022. https://www.theverge.com/2022/12/1/chatgpt-release-openai-explained

Vitali-Rosati, Marcello. "Digital Narration and Temporality." In *Digital Hermeneutics*, edited by J. Sinnreich and R. W. Gehl, 123–140. Amsterdam: Institute of Network Cultures, 2020.

Wells Fargo. "Wells Fargo Launches Internet Banking." *Press release archive*, 1997. Accessed May 2025. https://www.wellsfargo.com/about/press/1997/19971001/

WhatsApp. 2009. "Company History." Accessed May 2025. https://www.whatsapp.com/about

WikiLeaks. 2010. "Cablegate: 250,000 US Embassy Diplomatic Cables." *WikiLeaks*. Accessed May 2025. https://wikileaks.org/cablegate.html

Wikipedia. "History of Wikipedia." Accessed May 2025. https://en.wikipedia.org/wiki/History_of_Wikipedia

World Economic Forum. 2023. "The Future of Jobs Report 2023." Accessed May 2025. https://www.weforum.org/reports/the-future-of-jobs-report-2023

World Health Organization. 2020. "WHO Director-General's Opening Remarks at the Media Briefing on COVID-19 – 11 March 2020." https://www.who.int/director-general/speeches/detail/who-director-general-s-opening-remarks-at-the-media-briefing-on-covid-19---11-march-2020

Writers Guild of America. 2023. "WGA Contract 2023: AI Protections." *WGA.org*. Accessed May 2025. https://www.wga.org

Yahoo Inc. "A Look Back at Yahoo." Accessed May 2025. https://www.yahooinc.com/history/

Yamato, Jen. 2023. "SAG-AFTRA and WGA Strikes: The Battle Over AI." *Los Angeles Times*, July 20, 2023. https://www.latimes.com/entertainment-arts/business/story/2023-07-20/sag-aftra-wga-strike-ai-screenwriting-digital-likeness

YouTube. 2007. "Partner Program Overview." Accessed May 2025. https://www.youTube.com/creators/partner-program

Zakon, Robert H. "Hobbes' Internet Timeline." *Zakon Group LLC*, 2006. https://www.zakon.org/robert/internet/timeline/

Zendesk. 2009. "Customer Support Goes Hybrid." Accessed May 2025. https://www.zendesk.com/blog/human-ai-customer-support

Zoom Video Communications. "Zoom Video Communications Reports Results for Fourth Quarter Fiscal Year 2020." *Zoom Video*, March 4, 2020. https://investors.zoom.us

Zuboff, Shoshana. *The Age of Surveillance Capitalism: The Fight for a Human Future at the New Frontier of Power*. New York: PublicAffairs, 2019.
— *In the Age of the Smart Machine: The Future of Work and Power*. New York: Basic Books, 1988.

INDEX

Agency: 140, 142, 143, 158

Attention: 112, 116, 132, 145

Autonomy: 108, 109, 111

Belief: 64–67

Causality: 60, 69, 130

Choice-conditioning: 133, 135, 137

Credibility: 108, 110–111

Digital fatigue: 101, 104, 105

Dual self / Dual selves: 16, 24, 30, 110, 140

Epistemology: 57–61, 63

Fidelity: 44–48, 60, 63, 73

Infusus: 118–120, 123, 140

Interior integration: 110–112

Legibility: 46, 110

Ontology: 36–41, 44, 46

Perception: 60–63, 77–79

Phenomenology: 77–80

Pragmatism: 85–89

Presence: 16, 36, 38, 58, 60, 78, 140

Proxy condition: 1, 5–6, 9–11, 16, 36, 40, 57, 77, 85, 108, 118, 140

Recursivity: 11, 13, 43, 90, 118, 120

Self-authorship: 140, 143

Temporal jet lag: 99–105

Time distortion: 99, 101–102

Truth: 57–61

Value capture: 134, 137, 141

Visibility: 47, 109, 113

Voice authentication: 2, 8, 28

Volition: 144, 145

Witnessing: 77, 106

www.ingramcontent.com/pod-product-compliance
Lightning Source LLC
Chambersburg PA
CBHW060454030426
42337CB00015B/1584